You Can, Too...

A Personal Guide to the Divorce Process

The Little Grey Book
by

Rosie Woods

ISBN-13: 0692205810
ISBN-13: 978-0692205815

Copyright © Javin Press, LLC 2014

You Can, Too…
A Personal Guide to the Divorce Process
By Rosie Woods

Published By
Javin Press, LLC
118 N Alfred Street
Alexandria, VA 22314

'You must remember this- you are braver than you believe, stronger than you seem and smarter than you think.'

-- Christopher Robin

DISCLAIMER

This book is a personal account of my own journey through the divorce process. It reflects my personal feelings and advice as it relates to my personal experience. I do not claim to provide any advice that could be legally binding in a court of law. Nor do I endorse or oppose any particular cause or way of doing things. I intend no harm to anyone who may infer that I have made reference to him or her. Any statements reflected in the text are merely my own opinions based on my own experience. I wish you only good things!

~ Rosie Woods

ACKNOWLEDGEMENT

There are no words to express the gratitude I have for the people who have supported me in this journey – both through my lengthy and difficult divorce process, and the encouragement to write this book. My father and my siblings, my friends and support network, my amazing lawyer and my determined accountant, and my wonderful therapist. I am fortunate to be surrounded by so many incredible people.

To my creative partner, thank you for your unending love and support. You are undoubtedly the best thing to ever happen to me – I love you very much!

And to the reader, I "acknowledge" you wholeheartedly. I want you to know that you are not alone and I acknowledge your fear and pain. I wrote this book for YOU.

~ Rosie Woods

@RosieWoodsUCAN2 (Twitter)
Rosie Woods (Facebook)
RosieWoodsUCAN2@yahoo.com (Email)

FORWARD

The purpose of this book is to prepare you for divorce, whether you think you will be leaving your spouse soon, or at some time in the future. There are so many women out there trapped in an unhappy marriage with a controlling and manipulating husband. They have little or no access to the money, and they are subjected to any number of forms of abuse. While this book is intended for a primarily female audience, men in unhappy marriages will also find it useful.

I was stuck in a miserable marriage for over a decade. I didn't know what to do, how to get out. I wasn't equipped to save myself and take control of my care and future. I am living proof that I successfully divorced my husband. I am independent, self-sufficient and very happy. I survived a lengthy and stressful divorce process. **You can, too.**

Deciding to leave your marriage is a big decision. It is lonely. It is a decision clouded with shame and regret. You will need a great deal of help and you should not be shy about asking for it. I asked for help and to this day I am extremely grateful. My family and friends helped me with advice and support. They recommended and referred professionals. They took care of my children. They came and moved my belongings. And they lent me money. Asking for help shows good self-care. Care about yourself – you're worth it! You can always pay it back, or pay it forward. If people were not willing to help you, they wouldn't offer. There is no need to have any regrets. You are loved. Accept the help.

This book is my way of offering to help. It is intended to be small and discreet in size, but powerful and large in its message. *You Can, Too* should be considered a practical guide to the divorce process, not a self-help book to help you overcome emotional issues. It's meant to be your "go-to" book for divorce. Read through it more than once.

Highlight the points that stand out for you. Write down notes on the pages provided. Refer to the sections that apply to your current stage in the process. Keep it in your purse, or under your bed. Hide it from anyone that should not be aware that you are considering a divorce. It's meant to be your secret friend.

I was completely ignorant about how to leave my husband and what the divorce process was going to entail. When I asked my husband for a separation, I didn't care. I just wanted out. What unfolded for me turned out to be some of the most difficult, challenging, rewarding, and shocking months of my life. Much of what I learned is not anything that my friends or my lawyer could help me with. That is why I wanted to write down what I learned and share it with you. I have valuable insight and information to share with you. It was not easy to write this book since it brought back so many feelings and memories of a difficult period in my life. I just felt strongly that I had to write down what I learned so that others might benefit from my experience. I hope you benefit from the information in this book. I embarked out on a journey that now has a happy ending and I really want you to know that **you can, too.**

YOU CANNOT OPPRESS THE PEOPLE
WHO ARE NOT AFRAID ANYMORE.

~ CESAR CHAVEZ

Table of Contents

Figures

CHAPTER ONE:
UNHAPPY? – Start "Planning"

Life sucks. If you're reading this book, then you are probably pretty unhappy with your life. You feel lonely and ashamed – trapped. You get up every morning and the day looks the same. The mad dash to the bus, the breakfast dishes, e-mails and errands, what to make for dinner, soccer practice and homework, and then the husband comes home. It's never enough, never good enough. Something wasn't done right. Something wasn't done. The arguing. The silence. The tension. And the cycle starts over tomorrow.

Everything on the outside looks fine. You still hang out with the same friends, although you do less and less things as a couple, and more things with your girlfriends. Everyone has the same stress. Kids busy in too many activities. Teenagers testing the waters. You still make all of the family get-togethers. Your husband yucks it up with your brother and your father. Your mother gives you that knowing smile. It is what it is.

It doesn't have to be this way. You should wake each day feeling loved, useful and cherished. You should have fun with your husband and laugh a lot. You should feel supported. You should be having wonderful, close, nurturing sex each week. You should go to bed feeling happy and content that you have a wonderful life, surrounded by people who love you.

You are fooling no one. Your family knows. Your children sense your misery. They want you to stick up for yourself. They want you to be bubbly and happy and feel worthwhile. Your kids don't want to feel that they may be the cause of any stress (and, trust me, they feel it!) If you have to leave

1

the marriage to find yourself again, then that is what your children want you to do.

I know. You just want to get out – you want a different life, but have no idea how to achieve it. It's expensive, it's exhausting, it's embarrassing, it's shocking to some close to you, it's secretive, and it's time-consuming. Remember the big picture. You didn't get here overnight – you won't get out overnight, either.

It's worth it! I want you to get empowered and find your voice. Get unstuck! Just do it right; do it with as much class and dignity as you can muster. Do it gracefully for your children, but do it for your children, because – trust me – they hate what's going on at home right now. They know that you are miserable and have not been taking care of yourself. Your children **want** you to take care of yourself! Think about it, the people that we respect the most are people who take care of themselves.

It's time to break your silence and work through the shame. You are not a failure, just because your marriage is dead and over. You will actually find self-worth and success if you can summon the courage to get out of the prison you are currently in. First, talk to friends and family. Start slowly. Mention your unhappiness to your best friend, sister, or mother. They will offer advice – "make a list of grievances and talk it over with Tom", "maybe you need a (new) job?", "how about a marriage counselor?" If you're like me, you tried all of those things years ago. The changes made to everyday life with your husband only lasted two weeks. The job added new stress to your home life. The marriage counselor only had changes for *you* to make. Chances are, you never got real with the marriage counselor. Few spouses actually admit to what really goes on at home.

2

The courage to opening up these conversations really only helps the other people in your life get accustomed to the fact that you might be serious about leaving your husband. You previously never let on to his many faults, so they are only just now hearing about how awful he can be. Your friends and family are going to need time to adjust to the realities of your situation. Many of the people in your life will be shocked and surprised, because they only see the two of you out and about behaving properly. I honestly started that difficult conversation many times, without success. My mother and my aunt felt that we were having the usual marital discord of their generation. My other family members thought my husband was funny and adoring since he was always on his "A-game" at family gatherings (they didn't live with him). My best friend was so secure and happy in her marriage, I didn't think she would understand. And we had so many joint friends in the marriage that I didn't know who to trust.

One of the best ways to start reaching out is at a girls' party – or a charity event – where other women are already talking. Shimmy up next to a woman who is recently divorced and see what she has to say. She has been through the process and will be empathetic and discreet. A friend of a friend will offer plenty of advice and will probably keep your confidence. Start asking divorced women who they used for their lawyer. After they mention the name, they will inevitably have lots to say about whether it went really well – or really poorly! Be sure to write it down. Many names look and sound alike. Go home and Google the name and do some research. I loved my lawyer so much, that I passed out her business cards to anyone I ran across who seemed to need legal advice! Referrals will be your best source to securing a decent lawyer. And a good lawyer will be your best source to a happy financial future.

Ladies' events are also a good place to ask around for help with some of the other changes that are soon to come. You can meet other women who have similar childcare issues and might want to help you out. There are women who know of part-time jobs. There are bankers, doctors, investment brokers, mortgage brokers and realtors – all professions that you will need advice from. Friends and realtors will know of potential housing that you may need, if and when, you move out. I actually had a "separated, but living under the same roof" agreement. We told the kids we were officially separating and I began to sleep in a separate room above the garage. I had no idea how and where to move to. A realtor friend of mine knew that I wanted to move out, but didn't know how. She ran across a home for sale that had been on the market for a long time and the owners were considering a house sitter. It happened to be in my children's school district. I called a moving company and set a date. I moved out. It took tremendous courage. I lived there in that temporary house for eight months and it was perfect. The house was beautiful and close to the school. I didn't feel the stress of having to decorate and make it my own; I could just plain get used to living in a different location. It was perfect. You can find a housing solution, too. Just start by reaching out.

Like I said, it's scary. The fear can be incapacitating. Start slowly. Just mention your plight to people once in awhile where you feel your information can be safe. Take control slowly. Very slowly. You don't want to get ahead of yourself, either. If you haven't been independent for a long time, it can be daunting, but it's worth it!

Now that you have started reaching out for help, you need to also start hiding money. Every party in a divorce is hiding money in some way, shape, or form. You need to do it, too.

Ideally, you would have had your own checking account long ago, but I realize that this is not the case for the majority of women. So, go out to your local bank today and open a checking account solely in your name. Today. Put $500 from the joint account in it. When your husband realizes that you have done this, you can firmly say – with confidence – that all women should have their own account. All women should have their own checking account!

If you have a steady income and a trusted friend, you might want to ask them to open a savings account attached to one of their accounts and let you put money aside in that account. Only do this, if your can trust your friend implicitly!

You now need to syphon off some cash, wherever you can find it will go unnoticed. You can always get a certain amount of cash back from the check you write at the grocery store and it will just "appear" that you spent that much on groceries. Set aside $20 or $40 from each withdrawal you make at the ATM. Buy several items and then return some of them and get cash back. If you actually bring home a paycheck (vs. direct deposit), then get cash back from the bank when you make the deposit. Take a twenty-dollar bill out of your husband's wallet once in awhile. There are lots of ways to do it. You need to do it subtly in the areas that aren't under scrutiny from your husband. Start today. Twenty dollars here and there add up to hundreds of dollars over a matter of weeks. You will need every dime. And – despite what I said about having your own checking account – I want you to HIDE this syphoned money. For now, you can tuck it in an envelope in your sock drawer. Any money sitting in an account in your name will be subject to the divorce process called "Discovery" – the balance and transactions will be added to the outcome of the divorce settlement. I want you to have hidden, secret, emergency money that you will have all on your own.

It's important to determine (and often, discover) what is actually in your NAME. What bank accounts are in your name? What credit cards are in your name? What accounts are held jointly? What accounts are only in your husband's name? If you do not have any accounts in your own name, then it is time to have some. When you go to open your own checking account, you should ask the bank about applying for a credit card – in your name only! It is important to establish credit in your own name. However, if you already have a credit card in your own name, it's important to watch your spending on that card. Any positive cash flow in a bank account or investment account that is titled in your own name will probably be negotiated among the assets you split during the divorce process. Inversely, the debt that you have incurred (or do incur) on credit cards, property, or automobiles, etc. may follow you with sole responsibility during the divorce, unless you can somehow prove that it was debt incurred while in joint agreement. Once officially separated, you do not want to go out on a shopping spree and incur debt in your own name. It will follow you and you will regret it.

Similarly, I want you to have your own savings account and investment and retirement accounts. I realize that these are big steps. Every married couple should have their own retirement accounts. The tax ramifications and investment limits vary and you should maximize your potential to save for retirement. These accounts will be negotiated and settled in the "asset pool" during the divorce, but these separate accounts are important to your credit rating, and your independence!

First things first, you need to change all of your passwords. You need to prevent your spouse (and children!) from gaining access to your e-mail, social media, bank accounts and credit cards. Put your phone and computer on "lock" with a password, and do not use any of your old, obvious passwords that someone could figure out. Change the passwords on your frequent flyer miles and your other bonus cards, too. This may sound silly, but you don't want anyone else to use these things but you!!

Go to the Post Office and rent a P.O. Box. Start changing the address on your bills and personal correspondence. Tell your family and friends of your new address.

Go to the bank and look at the contents of your safe deposit box. Make a written inventory. Take out anything that is solely yours. If you have the need for it, go to another bank (where you now have your own checking account) and rent a safe deposit box in just your name. You can store your valuables and cash in the new safe deposit box for now. It's not likely, but be careful to remove cash or other valuables from this box prior to a subpoena of the contents. You will have to provide a written inventory of the contents of your box for the Discovery process, but the contents of your box can be changed by you at any time because it's only in your name.

Next, I want you to get familiar with your family's finances. If your husband is the sole breadwinner and pays all of the bills, my guess is that you are pretty ignorant of where all the money goes. It's time to get your head out of the sand. I wish that I had not been lazy in this regard. I should have paid attention to and respected the flow of money. I was unaware that my husband was making financial decisions without me. I was really in the dark about the financial infidelity!

To that end, it's important that you understand all of the accounts and all of the details – everything. You have THE RIGHT TO KNOW everything about the finances, whether or not you make the money. And the best place to start researching your marital financial picture is to get out your past five years of tax returns and find a quiet, secure place and read them. Compare them. Look at all of the schedules. Compare the schedules. Look at the interest you are claiming AND deducting. Look at the income. Look at the investments. Look at the deductions. If you don't understand what you are looking at, ask for help. I guarantee that you know someone who would be able to help you interpret your taxes.

I was intimidated by our annual taxes. We always filed an extension, and they were always prepared by an independent company and came in a package that was an inch thick. I didn't want to know. I wish that I had looked at them long ago. They revealed a variety of business investments that I had no idea existed (although, I was relieved that there was no tax fraud!). The reason that my husband always claimed that we had no money was because he was investing his paycheck in other ventures. I had no idea. A friend and a CPA helped me decipher our joint tax returns. I compiled spreadsheets and made comparisons between years, and I compared the investments with dates on the family calendar. It was important information. I learned critical information about my marriage. I became empowered in my divorce. I became empowered. Get out your taxes. Review them. Learn about them.

In a perfect world, the car you drive should be titled in your name, and your name only. This should have been the case from the day you got married, but I realize that not all couples understand good estate planning. If your car is paid off and the title is held jointly, then see if you can get your husband to sign the title over to you and get it changed at the DMV. You can say that your friends were talking about estate planning recently and you thought that might be a good idea (!). If there is a loan on your car, then change the title when you pay off the loan. If you get a new car, certainly title it solely in your name at that time! You and your husband should each have a car that is titled in your own names. If you can't accomplish this now, don't sweat it – it will be negotiated in the divorce. Just keep that in mind in the future.

One of the easiest and possibly most important things you can do now is move and/or secure your valuables. Inventory your jewelry. Take out an unnoticeable amount of coins from the collection. Pack up a few old books. Move your grown daughter's clarinet out of the house. Pack up and move anything that isn't on the radar that might be valuable. I want you to stop wearing your expensive jewelry and pack it up and put it in your new safe deposit box or take it to a friend's house. Out of sight, out of mind. Your husband probably doesn't remember all of the pieces that you have, nor has he been in the basement storage room recently. And you might have to sell some items to come up with some cash. You might consider calling your insurance agent and removing some of your pieces from your insurance policy (another way to get them to "disappear"). In general, your jewelry is yours and yours alone. Most items that your husband gave you would be considered gifts to you and then you, yourself, own them outright. Don't remove any items that are his family's heirlooms (unless his mother specifically gave them to you) – that is just not right. You just want to take anything that isn't currently noticeable

9

completely out of the picture – it's just that much less to come into play during the negotiations. And you honestly are more than likely going to have to sell some things to help with your temporary cash flow.

If you sell any of your jewelry – or other valuables - at this time, I want you to take the check that you receive and cash it and hide it with your other stashed away money. Continually take in sets of twenties to the bank teller (NOT at your usual bank location!) to get larger bills and then you will start storing hundred-dollar bills. You will be less tempted to dip into and borrow a twenty and you will be empowered and impressed as the hundreds turn into thousands. Stay away from your hidden cash pile!

Now is also the time to start cleaning up your act. I want you to stop – or curb – your bad habits. Stop the overindulgences. Stop overworking, stop overspending, stop drinking, and stop overeating. Control any compulsive behaviors. Clean up your e-mails, texts, and social media. Organize your paperwork. Clean up your finances. And, by all means, get rid of any extramarital funny business. You are going to want to present your best self during the divorce process and now is a great time to start being your BEST SELF!

A lot of what I am asking you to do is going to make you uncomfortable. It's scary. It feels "wrong". There is nothing wrong with taking care of YOU; it just feels strangely unfamiliar. My guess is that if you could put any of these propositions in third person, as if you were offering this advice to a friend, you would not have any hesitations whatsoever. It seems normal – a necessity – that someone else would take good care of himself. It should be normal for you to take good care of yourself, too! I guarantee that your ex-spouse is doing, or going to do, everything possible to take care of himself at the end of the divorce. I want you to do everything possible to ensure that you have an optimal outcome, as well!

Notes

_____

_____

_____

_____

_____

_____

_____

_____

_____

_____

_____

_____

_____

CHAPTER TWO:
THE DATA SUPPORTS THE STORY

It is critical that you collect, copy, organize and maintain the physical evidence that you will need for your divorce process. Every little slip of paper is important – every little slip of paper adds a detail of evidence that supports your claims. And some details that do not look important to you now may very well be important later. I cannot emphasize this enough. If you do not have access to some of the documentation, begin learning how to gain access to what you can.

First of all, both legal teams are going to ask you for financial records for the past five years. This means tax returns, paystubs, investment summaries, credit card statements, checking and savings account statements....If you are not already familiar with the process or the list, here is a checklist of things that you should be collecting and making copies of records for:

A. Past five years of tax returns with schedules and supporting documentation
B. Bank accounts (checking/savings)
C. Stock brokerage accounts, credit union accounts, money market/mutual fund accounts, stocks, bonds, certificates of deposit, thrift savings accounts or other investments
D. Credit cards
E. Mortgage statements and home equity loans
F. Car loans; student loans; outstanding notes
G. Retirement accounts
H. Pensions and trusts
I. Employment paystubs and W-2s
J. Current and previous real estate settlement sheets
K. Life insurance and annuity statements

L. Valuable items
M. Business partnerships and entities
N. Income from franchises, trademarks, gifts, inheritance, dividends, rents, pension payments
O. Health insurance; significant medical expenses
P. All other insurance policies
Q. Electronic data files of financial data (i.e., Quicken)
R. Items in a safe deposit box
S. Credit reports and histories
T. Appraisals and evaluations
U. College tuition payments for your child
V. Wills, trusts, Powers of Attorney, Medical Powers of Attorney

Educate yourself about the joint/marital finances. Often, one spouse usually covers the responsibility for "one aspect". My shame attacks were frequent and intense as I went through the details of our marital finances. I was so ignorant and unaware. I felt like I didn't have a "right to know" about income and expenses, since I didn't make the money. I was wrong. I had every right to know every detail. I was ashamed at how the money had been managed and the bills paid. I should have been a part of the financial process from the day we were married and I hadn't been, partly due to my own laziness, fear, and inaction. If you are like I was, and you are not up-to-speed on the state of your current finances, then you need to pull up your bootstraps and dig in. Put your fears aside and start to look at everything – the statements, the invoices, everything. It's time that you know every financial detail!

If an account is solely in your name, it will be easy to acquire these documents. If the account is held jointly, you can still gain access to the documents, but you might have to do some sleuthing to gather the account information. You have every right to access all information on joint accounts. If the statements are not readily accessible, then just contact the institution and make a request for access on your own behalf. Set up online access and alerts for every joint account. You will want to know immediately if your spouse is doing anything unusual with a joint account. While I do not recommend it – because it could set off a whole series of bad behavior – you can withdraw up to half of the balance of a joint account at any time. It is definitely best for your lawyer to advise you before you do this!

If the account is only in your spouse's name, then you will have to copy the records that you have access to before he realizes what you are doing. Take the records in small quantities and always return them to their original location, in their original order. Be discreet.

You will also need to go to your safe deposit box and remove items (if possible without them being noticed), or – at a minimum – make a copy of certain items and inventory the entire box contents. The bank can copy documents for you there at the branch. You will want to make this visit to the safe deposit box all in one fell swoop, because the bank keeps a record of each time you access the box and your spouse will know that you have opened its contents and when.

Enlist the help of a friend and spend a day at a copy store and quickly copy whatever records you have access to. The friend can help you undo staples and paperclips, and organize the piles to make things go more smoothly, because you have to make these copies quickly and then put them back where you had originally stored them. The legal process will require that the copies be single-sided, so whether the records and statements are single, or double-sided, go ahead and make the copy single-sided.

Copy everything, whether you think you need it or not. You never know when you might come across a transaction with a particular date on it, or something in your spouse's handwriting that could affect the outcome of your case. Go through the filing cabinets, collect the boxes in the attic and basement, and secretly scour his personal office! Sometimes, the documents are not actually required to be submitted to the courts, but might just refresh *your* memory regarding an event or a transaction.

Family calendars are important to keep track of, as well. They outline the specific dates and events of the past five years and they may help you piece together your spouse's pattern of activity (or absence). Often times, you will need to match up dates on the calendar with spending on a credit card or deposits into a separate account. All dates are important. Make separate notes of dates that mean something to you personally. I kept an on-going Word file of significant events and dates, as I discovered anything of note on calendars and statements. I was dismayed to find dates and sums that did not "add up", like my spouse paying more toward his credit card than paying toward mine, or a low balance in the joint checking account while at the same time, there was a high balance in an investment account in his name. There is no limit to the information you can gather and the more you organize and piece it together independently on your own, the less you will have to pay a paralegal for research and preparation. I kept organized binders with tabs that highlighted what I thought might be a potential issue in my divorce; and I provided all of the supporting documentation in one place for that issue to be resolved.

In my case, I took a friend to the copy store and spent two whole days copying my spouse's credit card statements. I learned a lot as I did the copying, briefly monitoring balances and transactions as I loaded the machine and sorted the copies into piles and folders. I also copied our joint tax returns and their schedules, as well as the supporting documentation that the accountant had used to prepare them.

I copied all documents relating to every house that we had EVER owned – realtor brochures, title searches, appraisals, and settlement statements. Everything. My spouse had purchased our first home before we were married. He wished to claim his down payment money – and subsequent interest over the years – in the divorce settlement. This meant that he wanted his original $40,000, plus interest over 18 years, to be reimbursed to him out of the financial settlement. It was difficult to prove the exact amount, since we had not only bought and lived in two other houses after that initial house, but had also refinanced several times. It didn't matter, though, since I *remembered* – and was able to locate and inform my lawyer of – the legal document we created when we did some estate planning where my spouse had deeded the title of the original home from him as sole owner to the both of us as a married couple. That saved a great deal of time and headache to solve that particular financial claim that my spouse was making. That was only one of many claims that would need to be tackled.

If you are tech-savvy and have access to passwords, make copies of all electronic files that you can. At the same time, *change all of the passwords you have that are currently protecting your information*. Electronic files can be both good and bad. A skilled accountant will be able to uncover all of the transaction history from an electronic download. My CPA was quick to point out where my spouse had recently zeroed out some previous commissions in his business account and "assigned" the money to another salesman in an attempt to hide money from me. Unless you are hiding cold, hard cash under your mattress, the money leaves a trail as it is earned, spent, and moved around.

Medical records are also important. They document both good (preventative) and bad (illness) medical issues. They add information to your timeline (if someone in your home was ill for an extended period, for example). They show expenses. They show history of claims.

It is important to remove any and all documents from a place of access to your spouse. If you are moving out, take all of the documents with you. When I moved out, I copied all of the documents that were only in his name and TOOK WITH ME all of the documents that were solely mine or had both of our names on them. I left all of the file boxes and folders empty right on the shelf where they were stored. It was much safer and easier for me to have immediate control and access to the documents myself, than it was to ask my spouse to give them to my lawyer or me later. Some of the documents, he might never recall to ask for and they could be used as a tactic in Discovery. In any case, I wanted him to ask me, not the other way around!

Store the documents that you are able to copy and gather in a safe place – at a family member or trusted friend's house. For added security, seal the boxes with a lot of tape. In the beginning of the gathering process, you will not need to research and go through these documents for a matter of weeks, so your primary purpose is just to gather, secure, and store the information for the legal process.

This won't be your last trip to the copying store. You will be making multiple copies of documents all throughout the legal process, but this is a chance for you to make a tremendous leap ahead. You may not have retained a lawyer yet. Your spouse may not yet know that you intend to file for divorce. Your lawyer is not going to encourage you to do anything potentially unethical and go undercover and copy documents that might be legally only his. The more that lawyers have to get involved with furrying out the documents and information, the more they get paid. This is for YOU, for your information, for your protection.

Both you and your spouse will be required to provide all of these documents during a process called "Discovery", so do not fret if you cannot gain access to some records that you realize are important. Your spouse probably already has "secret" information of his own, on his phone, computer, and at the office – do not worry. The helpful, critical part of gathering documents and records is to give you more time to mentally and physically prepare for your case. You will be ahead of the game in self-knowledge and organization. Be prepared to uncover some things in the documents that make your skin crawl, that incite you. Breathe. Keep plugging away at it, knowing that it will all be resolved eventually. The documents you pull together can help your lawyer prepare for the Discovery that you ask of your spouse, and begin to compile the folder of potential negotiation issues that will arise and are important to you. Gathering, copying, and organizing the records is just one more method of empowerment.

I also took all of the family photographs. I left a variety of photos in their frames around the house, but only after I had scanned and made a copy of them. The larger portraits, I took photos of with my camera and made a copy of them that way. The other photos stored in boxes – years of family memories – I took with me. If he asks me for them, I am happy to share. I am just glad that I do not have to ask *him.*

Throughout the entire divorce process, I kept a small date book in my purse and I made cryptic notes of daily activities, besides the actual scheduled appointments and events that happened. You never know when a small detail will be important to your case. You can code your entries to keep the information private. Make notes of where your kids were, whether your spouse was late, an important e-mail that you received, what you did, what you heard, what you felt, what you spent. It may have some significance later.

Notes

_____

_____

_____

_____

_____

_____

_____

_____

_____

_____

_____

_____

_____

_____

_____

_____

Notes

_____

_____

_____

_____

_____

_____

_____

_____

_____

_____

_____

_____

_____

_____

CHAPTER THREE:
MOVING OUT OR STAYING PUT –
Secure Your Belongings

It is difficult – on a good day – to move your residence. It is, indeed, difficult to separate and extract your personal belongings from a comingled life together. If you feel like you cannot move out because of finances, you need to think again. It is merely a matter of changing your view of "the finances". My spouse was continuously telling me that we "couldn't afford" a divorce. He was right in that "we" couldn't afford a divorce, but "I" could. I was willing to change my standard of living for the price of freedom and happiness; he just wasn't as willing!

If you fear for your safety, by all means MOVE OUT. Move to a safe location at a friend or family member's house until you can secure your rights legally.

In my case, I had already moved to sleeping in a separate room. My guess is that I could have stayed in that situation indefinitely – theoretically, until my spouse came home one day and announced that we had enough money to split our finances and set up separate homes. That was realistically never going to happen. There is never "enough" money to get a divorce.

And I am so glad that I did not force the issue and ask HIM to move out and stay in the house, myself. While is seems like a great idea, staying in the marital home is a whole other process in itself. You may be able to keep your children in their comfortable rooms, and known surroundings, but that is a ruse. Their home is no longer the same, once the separation occurs. And you will be the one running a (larger than you need) home all by yourself. You will likely be stuck with the day-to-day maintenance, the home repair appointments (since you don't want to give him all out access to the home again), the preparation for the sale and showings, the yard debris, everything. And you may have to live there on a temporary settlement amount (determined through the Pendente Lite process – see Chapter Eleven), which may be a great deal less money than you are used to. It definitely is easier in the long run to embark out on your own and start making a new home for yourself. It's just a whole lot scarier to actually move. And it's a lot of work to find a place to live and move your belongings to the new location. I understand that you are worried about your kids and their distress, but I want you to think about your self-care. I want you to think long-term about this decision. In this economy, it might take awhile to sell the marital home. Think about it.

The other thing about staying in the home and having him move out is that it delays the grieving process. You will be left in the home, surrounded by the memories of a life that once was. You will have to see the neighbors every day and pretend as though life is the same as it always was. And it's definitely not.

If your spouse doesn't know that you are thinking about moving out, there is a lot you can do to prepare before you DO tell him. First of all, take a photo inventory of the house interior and exterior. Photograph as much as you can. Open closets and drawers and photograph the contents. Keep this inventory in a private place. This is for your use, and your use, only. You may need to look back at the photos to jog your memory about something of value, or something in negotiations. However, you do not want the photos to be used to jog his memory, so keep this to yourself. It is for your protection only. And you may like to muse over the photos in later years to remember a time gone by....

Along the lines of photography, start making copies of any family photos and portraits that you want. Take the photo out of its frame and make a scan on your home printer. It is always easy to make reprints of these photos for new frames at your new house. Leave as many family photos as you can in place at the house. This is a kind and "nice" thing to do. There is a good chance that you will not decorate your home with all of these same pictures, and he will think that you went out of your way to send him an olive branch. Maybe he'll be less fired-up about the other things you take!

As I mentioned in the previous chapters, copy any and all documents that are *legally* only his, while you have access to them. This isn't terribly ethical, and in fact it's probably illegal, so be discreet. Make a copy of his birth certificate, his life insurance policy, his bills and credit cards. You may or may not need the actual documents, but you probably will need the information.

Pack up - and secretly move to another location – any items that would normally go unnoticed. Items stored in the attic and the basement is a good place to start. Take old antiques and junk that you might actually be able to sell and raise some cash. Take family mementoes and your children's childhood things. And take all of the photos that are stored in the boxes for safekeeping. Enlist the help of a friend and a truck and move out boxes and large items when no one else is home. Once you get the items into their truck, your trusted friend can move your stuff into a storage unit or someone's garage by himself or herself. Do this as often and as frequently as you can without your spouse noticing.

25

In a similar fashion, if you can get away with some credit card charges at places like Wal-Mart or Target, I want you to start shopping for - and stockpiling in a secret location - new household items to start furnishing your new place. You will need your own set of pots and pans, china, and silverware. You'll need laundry detergent and household cleaners, curtains and rugs, a rake, a microwave. Any time you can get away with buying something like this that will go unnoticed, you need to make the purchase and hide it away.

Take the dining and kitchen items that are seldom used. It's not likely that this will be noticed until the next holiday. Pilfer items out of "collections" – stamp collections, coin collections, book collections, and wine collections. Unless these have been carefully inventoried, a few items here and there will certainly go unnoticed.

If you envision the divorce process and settlement turning into something really ugly, take everything you want NOW. "Take now, apologize later." You have a slight glimmer of control over your belongings, if they are actually in your possession. You can bank on "out of sight, out of mind" for a good portion of them. And you can control the timing of what, how much, and when you give back anything you took that has stirred the controversy. That control is way more empowering than if the tables were turned and he had possession of something that you eventually want later.

By this, I want to suggest that you take "more", rather than what is "fair". The suppressed personality in a marriage has a warped sense of what is "fair", anyway. SO, I want you to take MORE than you think you deserve to take!

And take all of the historical records. When I moved out, I took all of documents that were carefully stored and packed away for each calendar year. I took the tax records, the mortgage and settlement sheets, family calendars, and the utility receipts. I took all of the documents out of the boxes, taking care to create a new organized filing system for myself, and I left the boxes back on the shelf at his house – empty.

What I am telling you here is not something that anyone else is going to tell you. And I am going to make the disclaimer here that I do not recommend that you do anything illegal. I am just trying to empower you to stretch yourself to protect your treasures. You can live with very little and be happy, but you can also live very well with everything that you can take! Be discreet in what you do, and be discreet for a very long time. Your children do not need to know; your family does not need to know. Your lawyer *definitely* does not want to know. No one but you needs to know what you took, or how you took it!

Notes

_____

_____

_____

_____

_____

_____

_____

_____

_____

_____

_____

_____

_____

_____

CHAPTER FOUR:
LIFE ON YOUR OWN

There will be much to learn about a new life on your own. Be patient and kind with yourself. Time takes time. You don't have to know everything all at once. Ask for help. Minimize your personal shame and embarrassment. It's a waste of time and energy. Instead, be brave and empowered and proud of yourself!

It's time to start managing your finances. And I mean manage. I mean look at them, know them, invest them, and protect them. There is definitely less money to manage, so make every penny count. Any time you lament the money that you don't have, I want you to remind yourself of the priceless freedom and happiness that you do have!

Start with your new personal checking account.
If you don't know how to balance a checkbook, go into your bank and meet with the Bank Manager. You can confidently go in and ask for help. Customers have trouble with their checkbooks and bank statements all the time. You don't have to try to figure it out online. Go into the bank and ask for help.

Extract your cell phone number from the family plan.
Negotiate your calling plan. Ask questions. Shop vendors.

Meet with your insurance agent.
Again, they meet with their clients all the time. Be sure that you have the proper insurance policies that you need in your own name. You might need renter's insurance (if you are now renting a home). You might need your own personal liability umbrella policy (if you don't know what this is, ask!). You will need your own auto insurance on the

car you drive and in your own name. Ask for discounts that they might be overlooking. They can run through a routine set of questions to help you navigate the policies. And start inquiring about health insurance. You need to get informed and educated. Your own individual policies will need to be disclosed on your income and expense worksheet, so get accurate insurance coverage and be sure to make note of these new policies on your monthly expenses.

Note: Be sure to always ask if there are any restrictions or ramifications to cancelling or changing an existing policy that you might have.

Do NOT make any changes to any life insurance policies.

Life insurance has value that will be negotiated and settled during the divorce process. Cancelling a life insurance policy could have significant impact on the divorce settlement. Once a policy is cancelled, you may not be able to obtain another policy like it, at that premium rate. This is VERY important – do NOT make any changes to any life insurance policies!

Put yourself – and your children – on a budget.

There is no shame in living on a budget. In fact, it is the most responsible, loving thing you can do. If you have never lived on a budget before, it takes effort and discipline. And it is incredibly empowering – not depressing! A budget gives you the chance to prioritize your life and live within your means and your core values. Take a careful look at your spending and see where changes might be made. Ask your children to start contributing for some of their expenses. Valuable life lessons are taught when children pay for some of the things they do or use. They have more appreciation and respect for their sports and lessons, their education, their car, and their phone. And there is no substitute for the experience of a part-time job.

If this is difficult for you, let me suggest this: change the way you communicate about money. "No" means "no." You don't have to rationalize anything. Just say, "I can't afford that right now," or "I am not willing to pay for that," not "your Dad doesn't give me enough money." State the facts. Ask questions. Are you sure that your child still *wants* that budget line item? Maybe they no longer want to play soccer. Maybe they no longer watch those cable tv channels.

And, speaking of children, start getting in the mindset that your children will be financially independent once they turn 18. I know that you want to give your children the best of the best in life, and support them in any way that you can, but you really need to get in the mindset of "launching' them into adulthood. And adulthood means earning a living and paying for their own keep once they reach the age of 18. You need to switch your mindset to self-care and independence. If you are overly generous with financially assisting your children right now, you might not be financially independent and prepared for retirement later. Do not be shortsighted about this. If it feels selfish, it is not. It is realistic. And it is good, necessary self-care.

Protect your assets.
Make solid, long-term financial decisions. Research and appreciate your investments. Make sure that you have a good financial advisor for your retirement and investment accounts. Look into current mortgage rates and home values. The value of your current home – or one you are considering purchasing – requires considerable research. Look at the costs associated with maintaining your home. You may want to switch TV/phone/internet providers. You

may need a new roof or HVAC system. If you are not going to be the one to exit the family home and instead are remaining in the house, make sure that you know what you are getting into long-term. The house may be difficult to maintain or sell in the future. You do not want to be "stuck" with it, and not be able to afford it.

Is your car a good investment for your current lifestyle?

If you have a luxury car or an expensive lease agreement, now might be the time to make a switch.

Research your health insurance thoroughly.

There is no cost to meet with an insurance agent and find out what is available to you. You can even go through the entire underwriting process without any charge. That way, there will be no surprises once your divorce is finalized. You need to factor health care costs into your final settlement. You deserve to have the same health coverage that you had in your married life. In many cases, you will be required to exhaust the COBRA coverage on your spouse's plan, but be sure to research and evaluate all of the options available to you. Be sure to negotiate who will be covering your children's health care during the settlement process.

Revise your Will, Power of Attorney, and Medical Power of Attorney.

Once you have hired an attorney for your divorce, inquire about having them draw up a simple will, as well as a new Power of Attorney, and a new Medical Power of Attorney. At a minimum, have your lawyer draw up new power of attorneys for you and – at the same time – send a letter to your spouse revoking your old ones. These documents give a trusted person control of your financial, legal, and medical affairs should you become incapacitated. And my guess is that you no longer consider your soon-to-be ex a "trusted" person.

Notes

_____

_____

_____

_____

_____

_____

_____

_____

_____

_____

_____

_____

_____

_____

Notes

_____

_____

_____

_____

_____

_____

_____

_____

_____

_____

_____

_____

_____

_____

Notes

_____

_____

_____

_____

_____

_____

_____

_____

_____

_____

_____

_____

_____

CHAPTER FIVE:
SELF-CARE – It matters on every level

On a realistic level, you are no good to anyone else, unless you are good to yourself. Self-care is critical. And, if you are not good at taking care of yourself, now is the time to start. Think of all of the people you admire and respect in the world – movies, politicians, people you come into during your daily travels – chances are, they look and act healthy. They are not overweight and bloated; they don't overindulge and do stupid things; and they seem bright and happy. You should be, too!

HALT. Hungry, Angry, Lonely, Tired.

These four things are the foundation for trouble. Watch for signs of these things and remind yourself to HALT. Stop the spin of any one of these things, and the chaos you are experiencing will likely recede. Hungry and tired are very easy to fix. Take the time to prioritize eating and sleeping during really stressful times. You'll reap the benefits tenfold. It's important. We tend to act carelessly when we are tired. We send regrettable e-mails, we overlook details, we trip on the stairs, we have car accidents, and we get emotional.

Your body needs rest. Ensure that you get adequate rest and relaxation (quiet) time. Plan for and stick to a regular bedtime. No late nights up worrying. If you need a sleep aid, seek the advice of a doctor. And while you're there, get a thorough physical. You need to be healthy. Also, take care of any nagging medical concerns you might have, however benign or insignificant. It is less expensive for you to get these things taken care of while you are still insured under the family policy.

Hungry is really easy to fix. No one wants to have a stomachache or be light-headed. Grab a banana, or eat a yogurt. Make a note to eat a decent meal in an hour. It will stop the "spin". Be careful, though, to watch your eating habits. Garbage in, garbage out. If you eat healthy fruits and vegetables and lean meat, your body will respond to the nutrients. If you make a regular habit of fast food, your body will respond with sluggishness. Make it count. If you are an emotional eater, this will be a hard time because stress can make you crave foods that you find comfort in. Try to manage the cravings. Switch to a lower fat brand of your favorite ice cream. Buy smaller chocolate bars.

Angry and Lonely are not as easily fixed as grabbing a snack or jumping into bed. Here you will really have to understand the importance of self-care and make the effort to reach out for help. Not so easy for many of us. Anger is a lack of compassion for yourself and you might need someone else to share in that compassion for you. If you can vent to a friend or relative to get those strong emotions out of you, you will find that once you get it off your chest, you will feel better. If nothing else, just ask them to validate you and empathize with you – they can *just listen*. They often will have advice, or be able to help you brainstorm ways to deal with the person or circumstance that is offending you. Your brain is only storing one perspective on the situation – and it's spinning it into something bigger and bigger. When you can voice your anger, the spinning subsides. You get a fresh perspective. Perhaps what you are taking as a personal assault really has nothing to do with you at all.

On a similar vein, if you feel lonely or alone in the world, you must seek out the company of others. You cannot expect other people to seek you out. They do not know what you need, unless you tell them. They cannot read your mind.

Force yourself to go out and be amongst the real world. Do not sit home and sulk and feel sorry for yourself. You have family and friends who love you. Go out and be amongst that love and support. They may assume that you are otherwise preoccupied or busy. Again, they are not mind readers. You need to seek out the company of others. Loneliness during time alone also leaves your brain to "spin" and lose perspective. "Woe is me" can be really overwhelming. Go out and stop feeling sorry for yourself.

The acronym, "HALT", is exactly that. When you are feeling really awful and overwhelmed, think of HALT – and STOP. Remedy any one of the four triggers – hunger, anger, loneliness, or fatigue – and I guarantee you will feel instantly better. Discover and develop appropriate methods to self-soothe. Call a friend, take a walk, watch a movie, or read a book. Factor in some time to adequately manage your stress. Consistently monitor your HALT and you will feel better long-term.

It is very important to try to stay in the present. If you spend too much time anticipating and catastrophizing what might happen in the future, you will lose sight of what is important now. Your kids are important. Their grades, their activities, the quality time spent with them. It is really important that you keep everything in perspective. The divorce is life changing and stressful, but temporary. No one is dying. You're going to be ok. Remember that!

Asking for help.
Contrary to what you may believe, no one is a mind reader. People do not know what you need unless you tell them. Again, it is not easy for most of us to ask for help. You need to get over that. Just because you are feeling shame and remorse over a failed marriage doesn't mean that you don't

need – and deserve – help. You would help someone in need. They can help you in your time of need. You wouldn't think twice about aiding one of your family members or friends. And you wouldn't put conditions on that assistance. Reversely, people want to freely help you. They wouldn't offer, if they didn't want to. If they offer, take the offer!!

You are going to need physical help. You need people to help you pack and move boxes. I had a friend with a truck come over during the day when no one was home to help me secretly move things out of the house to a storage unit. I had a friend come over when no one was home to help me sort through some of the difficult things to take. She helped me sort through the family china, the books and DVDs and the pictures. We laughed at some of the items and it was not lonely, regrettable, or stressful. I had a kind friend come and sit with me on moving day. The movers did all the work, but it was really nice to have someone there on such an emotional day. And I enlisted teenagers and men to help me with the brute force of large or awkward items that needed to be dealt with. You would be surprised how many people are willing to help. You just need to ask. Again, people do not know what you need, unless you tell them.

You need people to help you sort through and copy documents. You can give a trusted friend a box of documents that he/she can sort or copy in the security of her own home or copy place. Or you can do it together. Two heads are always better than one. I had a friend go with me to the copy place and remove staples while I threw my spouse's credit card statements into the copy machine and then we both collated everything and made piles. I had a limited time to have access to certain documents and I had to get the copies made. It was so much more efficient with two people.

40

You will need all kinds of other help, too. All you have to do is ask! You may need to find a new place to live, a new insurance agent, a new banker. You will need to start asking around. Family, friends, even acquaintances all know people who know people. I had no idea when I would move out, or where I was going to move to. A friend of a friend heard that I was looking for a place and set me up with a home that had been on the market for a long time where I could housesit for a few months until I could figure out what to do. I never would have had this opportunity if I hadn't started asking around.

Sometimes help comes from unexpected people or places. I didn't realize that I needed some help with furnishing my new home. Not every thing from a divided household can be split in two. A friend of a friend was getting rid of a rug, another friend had a kitchen table and chairs, and yet another friend had a dining room set! Even if these things are not to your liking, life is so much more simplified by having a furnished house during the time period that you are getting back on your feet. And you'll smile every time you go by, knowing that people love you and want to help you.

You will need professional help, as well. You might need to find a good therapist. You'll definitely need a good lawyer. You might need a banker, insurance agent, or a CPA. You'll need professional help with your taxes. You might need a consultant to help you decipher some of the things that come through in your spouse's Discovery. When my spouse delivered his Discovery documents, there were assorted business dealings that I had never heard of. I had to ask for help to determine what they were and what the potential value was!! Ask around. If you have friends in any of these professions, do not be afraid to ask for some free advice.

Lastly, you'll need financial help. Ugh. It is so difficult to ask people for money. I had to ask my elderly father and it was really, really difficult. He gladly gave me a large loan to pay my legal bills halfway through the divorce process. Without his loan, I would not have been able to keep up with the important work that my attorney was doing on my behalf. Divorce lawyers make you pay their bills each month. You cannot ask for them to be paid after a settlement is reached because no one really knows what the settlement will actually be. It's hard. You have to keep current with your lawyer to continually fight for a good settlement. If you have a good lawyer, it's worth the money. My settlement would have come out very differently, if I had not had the money to pay for the work that needed to be done.

The only thing that I can tell you about asking people for a loan is that you need to be prepared, organized, and logical about it. When you make your plea, state exactly what the money is to be used for and provide any supporting evidence that you might have for that amount. For example, send them a copy of the bill(s) you need to pay, or a statement of the work that still needs to be accomplished. Even if you need to borrow money for your kid's orthodontia bill, or your car insurance payment, send along the documentation to the person you are asking money from. Similarly, send along a simple document that acts as a promissory note. Unless the person is giving you money without conditions, you will need to repay the loan. Hand write or type up a document that outlines who gave you the money, the dollar amount, as well as the conditions for repayment of the loan (on such date, with potential interest, etc.), and sign and date it. Make a copy for you and the other person, as well as a copy of the check. Keep it in a safe place and make a note of any loans you have outstanding for your settlement sheet. It is very important to be business-like and professional about any loans you receive. No matter how close you are to the person making the loan, it is still money – their money. You need to be respectful and appreciative that they have trusted you and are willing to help.

As you can see, asking for help is a key aspect of appropriate self-care. We admire and respect people who take good care of themselves. We admire people who acknowledge their limitations. Acknowledge your limitations during the divorce process and take good care of yourself. The more you take care of yourself, the more care you can give your children, those around you, and your divorce settlement!

Use the Statement of Core Value.

One of the best pieces of advice that I used throughout my divorce process (and I still use periodically even now) was to use Dr. Steven Stosny's Statement of Core Value. I kept a copy of the Statement of Core Value in my wallet and I would pull it out and read it aloud when I was feeling particularly low. This statement is particularly cathartic when someone else (your spouse, your children, or even your lawyer!) is treating you poorly. If you feel disregarded, disrespected, unloved, inadequate or just plain lousy, read this statement aloud to yourself several times:

Statement of Core Value

I am worthy of respect, value, and compassion, whether or not I get them from others. If I don't get them from others, it is necessary to feel more worthy, not less. It is necessary to affirm my own deep value as a unique person (child of God). I respect and value myself. I have compassion for my hurt. I have compassion for the hurt of others. I trust myself to act in my best interests and in the best interests of loved ones.

SOURCE: Dr. Steven Stosny, PhD.
www.compassionpower.com

Notes

_____

_____

_____

_____

_____

_____

_____

_____

_____

_____

_____

_____

_____

_____

Notes

_____

_____

_____

_____

_____

_____

_____

_____

_____

_____

_____

_____

_____

_____

CHAPTER SIX:
DOLLARS AND SEN$E

During the separation process, it is important that you keep up your standard of living. This is not the time to live with less. You need to keep your expenses high and your income low (or none!). Why? Because you will want to portray that you still need to live in the manner that you were previously accustomed to when you were married. Your lawyer is not going to advise you about this. Ethically, they cannot tell you to keep your expenses high and live with "more" now, even though you are quite capable of living with so much "less". It's a "game". It's part of the long-term negotiating techniques. Take note. If your soon-to-be ex-spouse's lawyer or the judge appointed to your case sees that you can live on very little, you are likely to receive very little spousal support. So live large!!!

Now this is not as easy as it sounds. In fact, it's very difficult. Your finances and access to cash are limited. Your kids still make demands of you. And your legal bills continue to come due.... it sucks. However, if you have to rack up your credit cards to the limit or borrow money, you must do so. You will be required to provide a detailed summary of your monthly income and expenses during the Discovery process, and again, at settlement. This income and expense statement may also have to be substantiated by a history of monthly receipts. This is not the time to turn down the heat, or cancel a subscription that you can do without. This is the time to be creative with your spending. To keep your grocery bills "high", purchase less perishable items and more long-term things such as toilet paper, toothpaste and shampoo, or batteries. These things keep for years, and you'll be glad that you have them when you start to live on a budget.

At the same time – even though you are *physically* living large, I want you to start training yourself to imagine living with less. This means that I want you to take note of where you will be able to cut down your standard of living. Eventually, you will want to start putting on a sweater and turning down the heat. You will want to start shopping at the discount stores. You will want to cut back on your movies and dining out. You will have to live within your means. You will have to change your lifestyle. Nothing depressing about it – you'll have your freedom and happiness!!!

Be careful that you watch your credit cards very carefully. You want to make sure that you preserve your credit rating, so be sure to make timely payments of at least the minimum due. And when you eventually pay off your credit cards – and stop using them (!) – do not ever cancel a credit card. Keep your credit limit as it is, and keep your balance due at zero. Your credit-to-debt limit affects your credit rating. Keep the credit card with a zero balance, even though you don't use it.

While you keep your expenses high during the divorce process, I want you to start preparing yourself for the switch to less spending, once your divorce is finalized. Long-term, you are going to change your outlook on money. You are going to have to change your spending habits and your budget. Because soon there will be *less* money.

Now, here is the hard part. You need to have a serious turnaround with your mindset where your children are concerned. You have to really and truly come to believe that – once they turn 18 – they are no longer on your purse strings. Really! Of course, you wanted to pay for their college education. Of course, you wanted to buy them a car.

Of course, you are NOT going to do that. If you and your spouse had previously set up a 529 plan or some sort of savings for college, then that money should still be allocated toward that. If not, then any money that you are fighting for is to be *yours*. Yours. You earned it. It's yours. You are important. You have a future. You need the money, not your kids. At age 18, they can earn their own. And they will.

You need to have a talk with your kids and explain that things will soon change. You don't need to scare them, but you need to slowly and carefully inform them that they might need to now contribute to help pay for their expenses. I'm not talking about food and lodging (unless they are 18 and have graduated from high school). I'm talking about their cell phone, car insurance, gas, and clothing. These are all things that a normal teenager with a part-time job can help pay for. And they will appreciate it so much more, if they pay for it. Everyone can respect practical and pragmatic decisions.

Speaking of part-time jobs, if you can find a way to make some extra cash, all the better. I don't want you to go out and get a solid good-paying career job (because then everyone will know that you can!). But if you can make some extra cash by watching the neighbor's children, or something simple, it will be helpful to have the extra cash. I need to be very clear here. I learned from a friend's experience during her own divorce. She was a stay-at-home mother of three children and she decided to go back to a career, well-paying job. Because she became successful in the workplace, she lost her alimony because it was deemed "unnecessary". Perhaps she might have been happier with not working, retaining her spousal support and being able to stay home to care for her children.

Once your settlement is achieved, remember that your spousal support is YOURS – you do not have to justify ANYTHING about how you use it. Consider it your own money. It is similar to any employment income. You would not have anyone tell you how to spend your paycheck from the office. Do not let anyone have any say in how you spend your spousal support. There will be no guilt trips from the ex on this: "I give you all this money every month, you need to pay for Joey's cell phone." No. You get to make the decisions on how you spend that money, however much it is – or isn't.

I realize that we all have a certain amount of "baggage" when it comes to the finances. Some of us have unrealistic expectations, some suffer from entitlement, and most of us have worry and shame. I want you to clean up your relationship with money. It's just money! But money is what brings us the rest of what we so desire in life – safety, security, a roof over our heads, and food on the table. Take time to manage your money and show it the respect that it deserves. Take time to educate yourself about the best methods to manage your finances. It is time to learn how to save it, invest it, and budget it. Your life depends on it.

Notes

_____

_____

_____

_____

_____

_____

_____

_____

_____

_____

_____

_____

_____

_____

Notes

_____

_____

_____

_____

_____

_____

_____

_____

_____

_____

_____

_____

_____

CHAPTER SEVEN:
RESTRAINT OF PEN AND TONGUE

One of the biggest traps in life is saying something without giving it much thought. I am telling you to give every word that you say to your soon-to-be ex-spouse, and your children, some thought – lots of thought!!! So much of what we say is completely unnecessary. So much of what we say causes so much hurt and heartache. I am telling you that you can minimize the damage. Minimize the pain that is inflicted on your children. Minimize the miscommunication and reaction from your spouse. Minimize the cost of your legal fees. You need to train yourself to be less reactive, and it's not always easy. Instead of trying to mentally convince yourself of the benefits of restraint of pen and tongue, try *living* your way into new habits. Practice, practice, practice. Train yourself to NOT react. You'll be glad that you did!

Here are some simple tricks to help you learn the restraint of pen and tongue:

WAIT - Why Am I Talking????
This may seem obvious, but you will need to train yourself to *delay your reaction*. Delay your response.

Before you immediately reply to someone (and this works especially well with children), ask yourself:

"Does it need to be said right now?"
"Does it need to be said in two weeks?"
"Does it need to be said BY ME?"
"Does it need to be *SAID*?"

If you are having trouble with this, then start simply by saying "I'll get back to you." Or "Let me think about it." Both are non-confrontational, acceptable reactions.

If you are in the habit of over-functioning for others, this trick would apply to DOING things, as well – does it need to be *done* right now? Does it need to be *done* in two weeks? Does it need to be *done* by me? Train yourself to think realistically about the answer to these questions. Often, you will find that the issue will solve itself in a short time without any action on your part. I know that this might surprise you, but you do not always have to be in charge of the "answers".

Do NOT immediately hit the "reply" button.
In this current age of technology, we have grown accustomed to real-time, immediacy. Get accustomed to waiting. Train yourself to wait. Pretend like you're busy! Here is what you can do to avoid sender's remorse:

- Read an email and then close it. Just plain close it! Sleep on it. You can open it again whenever you want to, but let some time pass (at least an hour or two).
- Formulate your reply in a word-processor and then sleep on it. Have a friend review the content. It is safer to write your volatile thoughts down in a word-processor (or on a scratch pad). You can always cut-and-paste the content from a word processor into an e-mail correspondence.

You want to avoid hitting the "send" button before you really want to send it – and you certainly do not want to hit "send" before you are ready! If you practice this, you will be pleasantly surprised at how much mental effort you can avoid. So often, there is nothing that needs to be said. It may not have any value except to provide you emotional relief and there are plenty of less-harmful ways to get your own relief from angst. Trust me. It can WAIT.

Quit taking it personally!

Surprisingly, not everything everyone says or does is all about you. This is especially true concerning teenagers. If you feel insecure and reactive in this area, try to remember the "QTIP" acronym – and carry the actual Q-tip ear-cleaners with you. During one particularly difficult period, I had Q-tips in the kitchen, in my car, on my nightstand, and in my purse. They provided me with a constant reminder that I did not have to react to everything like it was a personal assault on my character. I have since decided in life that most things have little or nothing to do with me.

Treat your ex as you would like to be treated.

You cannot expect your ex to use common courtesy in his correspondence, if you are not doing so yourself. Always treat the person on the other end as though he is a business associate with whom you might like to do business. Always put your best face forward. Use a non-threatening topic in the subject line. Even if he *never* uses common courtesies, do not stoop to his level. Go ahead and establish some patterns and get in the habit of using them. Early on in my divorce, I put my child's name in the subject line every time I wanted to update my spouse with my child's schedule, grades, or other happenings. I just made it a habit and we both knew that it meant that the body of the text of the correspondence was solely about our child. I did not combine subjects. If I needed to also remind him to reimburse me for something, I sent a different email with a different subject line.

Use headings and salutations. Everyone likes to open an e-mail to "Hello" or "Dear", not just a directive statement like "what time do I pick her up?" It is a nicety that should not be overlooked. It is civil. It is nice. Treat the other person the way you would like to be treated – always.

Use "I feel…" statements.

Start any difficult dialogue with your ex using the "I feel…" statement. Only add "about…because…" if it is necessary. I feel…" is often enough of a statement. Elaboration is usually unnecessary. No one can dispute your feelings. No one can deny you from feeling that way. It completely removes any argument because you own the statement – it's all yours! Be clear with your words. Do not make personal attacks. Stick with stating your feelings, and only what you feel. Avoid starting a sentence with "You" and learn to start sentences with "I feel".

In a similar vein, you can interject "I feel…" in front of statements that you receive that seem to really annoy you. This might help you deflect your anger, frustration, and hurt. Instead of reading your ex's "You are…" and "You did…" statements and believing them, as written, try adding the "I feel that…" to the beginning of those sentences and reread the statement as your ex's *feeling* or *opinion*, not just as *fact*.

Review and revise.

Anything of importance should be prepared with care, and reviewed by someone else. You need to seek the confidence and advice of a friend or family member. You need someone else to take an objective review of the volatile issues that arise. Often, that trusted confidante will shed new light on conversations and can help you to see more clearly. Often, your friend will tell you NOT to send it.

It is important to use your sounding boards and professional advice. Be clear in what you are saying and asking for. Remove any emotional components. Do not make threats. Do not allude to past bad behavior. Keep to the facts, what is known to be true. Do not put anything in writing that is not factual. Have someone else proofread it and take their advice on any improvements they suggest. You want to avoid any regrets in the future and if it is in printed word, you are not going to be able to take it back. It's there for perpetuity, especially if it is on the Internet!

Stay organized.

An organized life will also keep your mind organized. If your files are in disarray, then so will be your thoughts. Keep your e-mails organized in folders. If you need to worry about privacy, name the folders something benign and unrelated to the divorce. You may need to keep folders separate regarding your children and issues that arise specific to them. Keep dialogue with other people in similar folders. It is important that, when you need to quote or refer to a particular correspondence, that you can find it. You can also forward e-mails to a friend or yourself, if you need to.

Keep a copy of all snail (post office) mail and voice mails. You may need proof of what was said and you will need to document the date and time. Be sure to back up the data on your phone regularly.

Be discreet.

Make sure that you have your own e-mail address. There are lots of sites that give you free access to e-mail accounts. Do your best to ensure your privacy. Do not give out your passwords. Close your email account if you walk away from your computer. If you share a computer, partition the computer into separate login accounts, so that no one has access to your documents and spreadsheets.

It is imperative that you do your best to shield your children from seeing or overhearing anything about the divorce process. Put away the papers and computer files. Close the door or leave the house to have a conversation. Leave the room or the house, if you need to collect yourself. Even a partial conversation can lead them to worry or misconstrue details. They have enough on their plate with all of the changes. Be sure to shield them from all details. It's none of their business.

Relinquish control – find serenity and strength in the powerlessness.

Much of what is going on is entirely out of your control. Think about it. If you are obsessing about someone else's actions or behavior, you really are powerless. You cannot change someone else. You can ask or remind, but after that, let it go. You work on what you have control over, and you need to let go of the rest. If you can ask yourself, "Can I do anything to change this situation?" and the answer is "No", then just stop thinking about it. If you have trouble letting go, I suggest that you create something like a "God Box". Get a shoebox, and put it on the top shelf of your closet. Write down on a slip of paper (wherever you are, whatever you are worrying about) or print out a difficult email and place the paper in your God Box. Let it go. Something about the ceremonial aspect of writing it down and placing it in another location allows you the freedom and release to actually let it go. It works. Try it. Some day, you will then look in the box and realize that it was taken care of, however it was taken care of, and that all is right in the world. Some of the slips of paper might even cause you to chuckle. And why was I ever worried about *that*??

Remember that the written word is forever held in posterity. E-mails, texts, social media, and printed documents are all kept "forever" now. There is no escaping what you have typed into print on any media. You can't always burn or shred or hit the delete button anymore!! You have to think before you say anything that might harm you or someone you love. Don't send any emails that you don't want to see thrown back in your face. No nasty language of any kind. Be direct. Be kind. Use careful thought and editing. Don't leave any room for misinterpretation. When you want something – or don't want something - be succinct and direct. You don't need to embellish, you don't have to give reasons, or details. And remember that "No." is a complete sentence. Consider every issue a business transaction – void of emotion, all business. Win-win.

Think about it in real terms. Is it easier to walk forward, or backwards? Doesn't it take twice the time and energy to retrace your steps and move in a different direction? I like to think of what my high school softball coach taught me. I played center field where those long high fly balls come and they often went over my head. Finally, my coach instructed me to take one big step backward just as the batter was hitting the ball. We would do multiple drills of this with my coach hitting fly balls to me over and over again. Sure enough, as I learned to – first – take a big step backward, I could then position my body and concentrate on the height and direction of the ball, not go into panic anticipating the ball as I heard the crack of the bat. I could then adjust left or right, back or forward. And I usually caught the ball! Use this same concept in your daily communication. First, step back from whatever emotion the communication might trigger in you. Then proceed in a "forward" pattern with a thoughtful, calm response. Forward movement is the intention, not

missing the ball entirely by letting it go over your head, and
having to redirect your play.

Notes

_____

_____

_____

_____

_____

_____

_____

_____

_____

_____

_____

_____

_____

_____

_____

Notes

_____

_____

_____

_____

_____

_____

_____

_____

_____

_____

_____

_____

_____

_____

CHAPTER EIGHT:
PROTECT THE CHILDREN – ALWAYS

In some states, the court will mandate that you attend a co-parenting seminar. Because of the far-reaching bad behavior of some parents caught in the middle of a divorce, state governments are now trying to be proactive. In my case, I went for a half-day class and I submitted my signed attendance certificate to my lawyer. I also had to go watch a 30-minute movie at the local courthouse. Judges frown on bad parenting. It's not rocket science. Good parenting is a reflection of you as a whole. You should always present your best self – especially when it comes to your children!

Kids should never know what you, or your spouse, are doing – EVER. Kids respect (and are taught self-respect) by those who respect themselves. Self-care. Take care of yourself. Eat right, shower, exercise, act respectable, act the way that you want your children to act, now, and when they are older. You will NEVER unleash what you really think of your ex – what they did, how awful they are. Kids need a father and a mother, and they will form a relationship with each of them of their own doing. What happened between the two of you, happened between the two of you, not because of anything your kids did. So keep it between the two of you. The kids will find out enough details on their own, eventually – and it will possibly hurt – but it won't be because YOU hurt them by telling them. You need to keep your side of the street clean.

I implore you to not be short-sided about this. You will command long-term respect from your children and other people by not divulging dirty details. You do not need to sway anyone to take sides. You need to shield them from the entire process. This is for the long-term. Forever. No one needs to know what your ex did to you, except you.

During the periods of time where the paperwork is the main focus, you will need to keep the piles of paper organized and out of sight. You need a workspace that is separate from the living area of the rest of your family and you need to pack up everything in boxes with lids when you are not working on them. Stay organized, but stay discreet. Purchase file folders and storage boxes from an office supply company and create a filing system that works for you. Conceal and cover up any documents that you need to keep readily available. I want you to be extra careful with sensitive documents such as anything that references the children; any motions filed by either lawyer; or any financial statements that portray balances or wealth. Any angry language or incorrect or partial financial data could be very hurtful to an unknowing party. It is imperative that you avoid the dissemination of any misinformation.

Another thing that you must consider is the frequency and intensity of certain periods of the divorce process. Try to maintain an "even" façade for your children. Try not to leave your phone unattended. Even if you have it locked with a password, missed calls are often identified on the outer screen and can be viewed by anyone. Similarly, unopened mail left on the kitchen table can be alarming, if it has return labels from law offices or certified green stickers on it.

I also want you to keep your emotions and exhaustion under wraps. Be sure to engage in conversations that are private. You do not want your children to overhear you talking to a friend or neighbor, and you definitely do not want your children to listen in while you talk strategy with your lawyer. Leave the room, or leave the house. Make sure that you cannot be overheard.

If you have a lot of energy and work to put into your case, I want you to leave the house (or make sure that your children are not home). Do not let your children be exposed to the number of hours you spend on the paperwork, or your volatile emotions to the current problem. They need to see that you are "ok" – that everything is going to be "ok". The divorce process should not be a frightening experience for your children (even if you are fearful yourself, at times!).

You also might need to "ease into", or cover up any of your "new" behaviors. Sudden changes in behavior can make children uneasy. Keep your new daily planner in a private, safe place and encode any notations that you want to keep private. Ease into a new daily routine. Enforce a new budget over several months. Introduce new friends and acquaintances in a limited fashion. If you have to make a lot of changes at once say, because of the move in or move out, then try to make other changes that you want or need to make over time. Prioritize the disruptions that you make to your children's schedules. Be kind. They did not ask for this huge, all-inclusive disruption!

It is not always easy, but you and your spouse need to find a real-time, decent way to communicate about the children. Your children come first – always. They deserve to have two loving and caring, involved parents. That is their birthright. You both need to – and have every right to – know how your child is acting and feeling, what he/she is doing, his daily schedule, who she is spending time with, etc. And you both deserve this information in a timely manner. If you are the holder of this information, you need to act as a loving, responsible parent and get the information to your ex. E-mails are quick, timely, and can be void of emotion. State the facts, as you know them. Ask for co-parenting help, if you need to. Do not rely on your children (of any age!) to convey or translate information for you. Details can be overlooked or misinterpreted and emotions and ideas can be wrongfully portrayed. It is cowardly of you and unfair to your child to lay that responsibility on him.

Gather your courage and maturity and establish a communication routine with your ex that covers all communication about your children. Think of your children as a business and try to communicate with your ex the way you might deal with a business associate. Make careful consideration of things that you would generally want to know and do your best to inform the other parent. To remove any volatility of such conversations with my ex, I would always write the Day and Time of Day (i.e., Wednesday morning) in the subject line. That way, he would know that it was something about the kids and that it was Wednesday morning. I only followed this pattern, if it was routine information about the kids. After awhile, the pattern developed a non-threatening rhythm and we could both feel comfortable that the content of the e-mail was important, but not generally difficult or volatile.

In an ugly, difficult divorce where there is a great deal of bad behavior and miscommunication, you may need to avoid your ex and set up a direct line of communication with the source of information. Most people are familiar with dealing with divorced parents. Place a call or send an email and ask to be added to the distribution on any communication from the teachers or coaches. Make sure that you receive copies of all school progress reports and school schedules and activities. Ask for a separate copy of the church or club newsletter. Make sure that you are included and up-to-date concerning any medical or emotional issues with your child, regardless of which parent is paying the medical bills. Therapists, by law, have to notify both parents when they are counseling a minor child. Until your child turns 18, you have every right to go directly to the source of outside information. Just kindly ask to be added to their method of communication. You do not need to go into any details, just be gracious and kind.

If your child is old enough, you can ask them direct questions about their grades, friends, and schedules. Don't be frustrated or angry about it, just show a genuine interest in their lives, and glean as many facts as you can at the same time. Even if they only know that they have a game on Saturday, but don't know what time or what location, you have enough information to gather from other sources the information you will need to show up at the game.

Parental alienation should be avoided at all costs. Your children should remain neutral. All children need two parents in their lives. You want them to love each parent equally, and unconditionally. You do not need to taint their views of the other parent with your own views. Keep your own perspective and opinions to yourself!! You do not need to engage in bad-mouthing or disparaging remarks; you do not need to embark on any sort of "competition" for your children's time or attention; you do not need to protect or prevent them from experiencing the other parent. It is what it is. They can develop their own opinions about and relationship with their other parent. They don't need you to over-function or meddle in any way. It is counter-productive and you skew (or prolong) their reality. It is important that your child have a relationship with the other parent, however good, bad, or indifferent. They cannot have a relationship, if they do not have any interaction.

If you are struggling with your relationship with your child, you would want your ex to be encouraging and supportive of you, not antagonizing and disruptive. Always stay on the right course and do the next right thing. If you don't know what to do, do nothing. It will come to you. Use "I feel" statements, not "You should...". Listen, and listen some more. Hone your listening skills. Validate your child's feelings and always empathize. Make yourself available. Stick to your family values. Ask for a "redo". Any hour or day can be started over. Apologize, when necessary. Just do the right thing by your child. You will reap the benefits over and over again – now and in the future.

Do not introduce a romantic relationship into your family life at this time. Do not!! Romantic endeavors complicate everything. I know that you might be lonely or insecure, but you will need to seek the solace of family and friends right now. Not only does an intimate relationship with a member of the opposite sex cause all kinds of ramifications in your legal process (specifically, you run the risk of forfeiting your alimony!), you will find yourself in all kinds of other trouble. If you have to sneak around, chances are you are spending a great deal of valuable time and money to do so. And you do not have a surplus of time – or money – right now. You need to give all of your spare time to your children (and the divorce process).

A new relationship right now also clutters and befuddles your mind. You cannot think clearly about your future and you may not make solid, long-term decisions that are in your best interests. You may be physically and emotionally satisfied temporarily, but you will also experience long-term shame and guilt and remorse. If you have to be covert and "sneak around", then you are not exhibiting respectful behavior; you are lying and cheating in the same way a criminal acts. If the attraction is meant to be, it can wait until your divorce is finalized. Your children will most likely learn to love and accept a new person in your life if he or she is introduced to them in a temperate, appropriate way, much in the same way that you would want your children to introduce someone to you!

The best thing you can do for your children is to be available to them. Just your presence alone provides them with security and comfort. Try to keep their schedules and routines as normal as possible. Make sure that you follow through on your commitments to them. Be reliable and accountable. Try to just "be". Try to listen more. Try doing nothing. Often, I would just cook something or bake cookies in the kitchen to make myself present and unassumingly available in the center of the house. It gave my children the opportunity to start a conversation with me, if they wanted. Or they could just do their homework at the table and be near me. I also had to "busy" myself with other projects in the main part of the house or watch television programs that I thought were horrible in order to foster an opportunity to engage with my children. It takes effort, but it's worth it!

Notes

_____

_____

_____

_____

_____

_____

_____

_____

_____

_____

_____

_____

_____

_____

_____

_____

CHAPTER NINE:
YOUR LEGAL TEAM –
Maximize the effort, minimize the spending

Naturally, it is important to hire a good lawyer. You want one that is going to "win" your case, plead your side, and understand your goals and conditions. The best way to find a good lawyer is through referrals. Start asking around. Ask your girlfriends. Find someone recently divorced, or going through a divorce. Everyone knows someone – and they know if they are good, or if they are bad!

My lawyer came highly recommended by a friend. And I recommend her now to everyone I know. She was sharp, and she was expensive. She played a mean game of poker, and she turned all the legal screws (which is fair play, by the way!). Together, we researched and covered every angle of my case. I helped her prepare by keeping her up-to-date, and informed. And she helped me by handling the legal ins and outs to obtain a fair and proper settlement.

When you secure a referral, give that law office a call and set up an appointment. Be discreet about making the appointment. Only use your cell phone, and mark the date in your book with a nondescript code. If you choose to hire the lawyer that you meet with, take whatever cash you can part with and sign a retainer form. This secures your legal team in place, but does not leave a "trail" until you are ready to inform your spouse of your intent to move forward. The retainer fee is usually several thousand dollars, and the contract that you sign is fairly robust. It can be rather frightening. If you have any questions about how to handle the retainer, ask. You might be able to negotiate your retainer fee down. Your lawyer merely wants to ensure that he or she will be paid, irrespectively of how the settlement goes. The retainer monies are kept in your account; the money doesn't actually pay your monthly legal bill for services rendered. The retainer is used to fund any out-of-pocket expenses that your lawyer incurs, such as advice from other professionals (accountants, consultants, etc.), court reporters/transcribers, and subpoena services. And you will have to replenish your retainer back to the set amount each month, as well. When your case is settled and all legal details are finally complete, your lawyer will refund the remaining balance to you.

So – to be clear – you need to pay your lawyer up front a set amount of money to keep her working for you (to "retain" her services). If she uses some of this money to pay for expenses incurred outside of her office, you will need to replenish that money (called "client funds") each month. IRRESPECTIVE OF the retainer, she will send you a monthly bill each month highlighting the time increments that she has spent on your case, a description of what she did with that time, and a cost for that time that she spent on you. And, at the bottom of the bill, there will be a total for the amount due. That total will be the sum of the client retainer funds to be replenished and the amount for the services that she, herself, has provided. Do not be shocked – it's expensive. Lawyers went to law school and took the bar exam so that they can now be compensated at a high hourly rate. And they can charge that rate because they have a client base that keeps them busy at that rate. Good lawyers can charge a high hourly rate, and they are worth it.

Your referral should direct you to an honest, ethical lawyer. And your gut instinct will help you with your remaining anxiety. One thing to watch for, though, is a lawyer's overhead. Is the lawyer you are considering a partner in a large firm? Does he/she turn over the mundane work to lower-level associates? Does he work in an office in a high-rent district? These factors could contribute to a higher hourly rate, also, and that may not be in your best interest. Another factor to consider is whether or not your lawyer is willing to actually go and argue your case in court, before a judge. Some lawyers prefer to litigate via documentation only, and cannot handle the real-time drama of a case with players on the stand in front of a judge. It is important to make sure that your lawyer is skilled and willing to go the distance and defend you in court. You may not actually end up in court (you may settle the case in mediation), but you need to be prepared to go to court, if necessary, and you want the best presence in court that you can.

So, now that you have met and contracted with a lawyer that you highly regard, here are some tips to help minimize that monthly bill:

Always consolidate your correspondence. Any time that your lawyer answers the phone, opens your e-mail, or meets with you, it costs money. If she charges $400/hour, for example, she may charge you $100 for the 15 minutes that it takes her to open your e-mail, read the contents, reply or not reply, and file that information away. A hundred dollars is a lot of money, and it adds up to thousands pretty quickly. Find someone else to hold your hand. Find a friend to vent to. And see if someone else can answer your question before you ask your lawyer. You know a variety of people in a variety of professions and experiences – use their free advice and consolation as much as you can. Utilize a variety of sounding boards. Keep your contact with your lawyer legal and relevant. Only meet with your lawyer when you have to actually prepare for your case. Type up notes and questions into an on-going Word file, and then cut-and-paste all of that text into one e-mail. By consolidating your contact with your lawyer, you are conserving time and energy on all fronts and that equals money.

Remember that your lawyer has other cases and other clients. He or she may not be able to get back to you right away. Continuously "pinging" your lawyer while you wait for a response is counter-productive. As I stated above, your lawyer charges you every time he answers a call or opens an email. Be patient. Your lawyer is very aware of the deadlines surrounding your case. He will get back to you when he can.

Ask to make your own copies and deliveries. My lawyer allowed me to come to her office and pick up documents that needed to be copied and/or delivered to my spouse's lawyer. The documents always need to be copied for your own personal needs, that of your lawyer's, and the legal requirements for the opposing lawyer. A law office is going to charge for the office staff's time, as well as the office copier's inflated per-page rate to copy documents. Your time is free, the copiers at printing centers are cheaper, and you can put the cost of the copies on your credit card (vs. having them added to your lawyer's bill).

Another benefit to making your own copies is that it forces you to (however briefly) look at the papers you are copying. Often, when I was making my own copies, I would come across entire documents, or select pages of a statement, that looked foreign or unusual to me. I made note of it and revisited that document later to look over any details that might be important. If someone else had made the copies for me and just put the copies in a box, I might not ever have reviewed, or even seen, certain documents because it was overwhelming and I did not know what to look for. Sometimes the smallest detail would catch my eye – a vendor name, a date, or amount – and I was able to point out something new of relevance to my lawyer.

Small documents can be faxed or e-mailed, but large boxes of documents need to be mailed or delivered. Personal delivery services are also fairly pricey, so see if your lawyer will entrust you to make the deliveries yourself, and you'll save some money there, too. Always be sure to obtain a receipt for any documents that are coming or going, either for copying or delivering. You need to always be sure to keep good records.

Stay up-to-date and on top of your case in an organized manner. The more prepared and organized you are, the less time and money you have to spend on someone else's efforts to pull all of the information together. Keep a journal or log of important dates or details. Input data into Excel or Word, so that you can sort it later, or use it to cut and paste into other pertinent documents. Maintain organized files with labels that show accounts and dates. Put subject matter in chronological order.

Begin to make a spreadsheet inventory of items that are to be divided. For each item on the list, make a column for:
- Its estimated (or known) value
- Your suggestions on the optimal division of the asset
- Options that you would consider negotiating
- Any emotional factors associated with the asset
- Note of any supporting documentation

If you do not already have access to online visibility to your various bank accounts and credit cards, now is the time to gain online access and download monthly and annual summary reports of all transactions. Save the files electronically on your computer. Locate, copy, and maintain organized boxes of the necessary documents that were mentioned in Chapter Two. This will take a great deal of time and effort on your part. It can be emotional and exhausting. Do not be discouraged. Ask for help (*free* help!). The more time and energy that you spend to organize the documents and information you need for your case, the less money you will have to spend on that same effort being done by someone else.

Get educated.

You're smart. You have the wherewithal to begin this process. Now, put your best foot forward. Gather all the – common – knowledge that you can from friends, acquaintances, and other professionals (vs. your lawyer). If you do not understand balance sheets, ask someone who knows to explain them to you. If you do not understand the ins and outs of real estate transactions – appraisals, settlement sheets, mortgage insurance, etc. – meet with a realtor and learn what all of the terms mean. Learn how to read investment summaries and the complexities of retirement accounts. You may need to decipher Articles of Incorporation, Stock Options, and the make up of LLCs. Review and understand – *really understand* – your tax returns. It is important to decipher the various Schedules and deductions because these may end up being points for negotiation. Set up an appointment with your (or a new!) insurance agent. You need to fully understand all of the insurance issues, as well as know what insurance you may need in the future and the specifications and finances that might be required to secure that insurance. If you are making a claim for spousal support (alimony), it will be important for you to own a life insurance policy on your spouse. Seek the advice and counsel of an accountant because there will almost certainly be tax implications as part of your overall settlement, as well.

Frequently, receipts and documents will appear throughout the divorce process (especially during Discovery) that will downright look foreign to you. Overcome your fear and ignorance and seek out knowledge. Request as much free and inexpensive help that you can to educate yourself. Do not pay your lawyer for the time to explain things to you that you can otherwise get from someone else. Initial consultations with most professions (real estate and insurance agents, CPAs, investment brokers) are free at no cost to you to go in and make inquiries.

In basic terms, start to gather knowledge for living. Your spouse may have always handled certain aspects of your marital life, and now it is important that you understand ALL aspects of your daily life, partly for your divorce proceedings, but mainly for embarking out on a life of your own. You do not want to end up being newly single, and discover that there was some aspect that you could have thrown into the divorce settlement, but you just "didn't know".

Educate your lawyer.

Your lawyer needs as much information about your case as you can possibly give him or her. Beside the basic factual information, you will need to provide your legal team with anecdotal information for them to gain some perspective on the important factors of pleading your case. It is wise to type up a summary sheet of your life that outlines past events and highlights milestones. An accurate outline in written form proves to be a good guideline for you and your lawyer to refer to during the divorce process. Type up – and then massage over time – what your desired outcome of the divorce is. Think in terms of one year from now, five years from now, and twenty-five years from now. You have to come up with realistic terms that you are looking for to protect your family, you personally, and your finances and assets. "I just want out!" doesn't tell your lawyer what you want to be "in" the rest of your life.

It is critical that you describe your spouse accurately to your lawyer: how he operates; what he views as important; his lifestyle and spending habits; his family of origin; his parenting style; his place of employment; his values and interests; and any emotional triggers. All of this information will help your lawyer manage your case. A good lawyer will know when to – or when not to – use this information to create a good case for you. This is part of your offensive plan. This is where you maneuver low blows at his weaknesses. This is where you hold your trump cards that you keep close to your chest. The more accurately you can describe your soon-to-be ex, the better equipped your lawyer will be to negotiate your settlement.

Notes

_____

_____

_____

_____

_____

_____

_____

_____

_____

_____

_____

_____

_____

_____

_____

_____

Notes

_____

_____

_____

_____

_____

_____

_____

_____

_____

_____

_____

_____

_____

CHAPTER TEN:
THE "GAME"

There are aspects of the separation and divorce process that do not seem like a good idea and – long-term – they are not generally good ideas. It's all part of the "game", the dance, the web of make-believe and pretend. A lawyer cannot ethically advise you to *pretend*. He or she wants everything to be legitimate, realistic, and *real*.

I am going to tell you what no one else is going to tell you because it involves not being nice and not playing fair.

You are going to need to pretend that you need a lot of money to live on. You are going to pretend that you do not have a great deal of earning capacity. You are going to over-emphasize and exaggerate things – with legitimate proof. It's all part of the game, "Poor, pitiful me." I guarantee that your spouse is playing a version of this game, so I want you to buck up, throw your reservations to the wind, and bring your badass self to the plate.

First of all, I have talked about making sure that you keep your cost of living high. That is, keep spending money the same way (or more) that you have always done. You need to look and act as though you *must* have the accommodations that you always had. Even though you are able to cut down on some of your expenses, do not make any cuts right now. And you need to be able to provide proof of your spending. SO, keep your grocery bill and your dining bill the same, but skim cash off the top where you can. Have a friend pay you cash for his half of the restaurant bill. Take cash back from the grocery purchase. Buy less perishable items at the grocery store and buy more sundries (they will turn into an investment later for your more frugal life!). If you normally use a check or credit card for everything, then I want you to still do that, but I also want you to take out cash from the ATM. Most people take out cash from the ATM several times a month and they don't normally account for how they spend it. I still want you to use your checks and credit cards for things you normally buy, but I want you to take out reasonable amounts of cash once in awhile from the ATM and NOT spend it. I want you to sock it away and save it – you don't have to account for that "miscellaneous" cash. If you are accustomed to using cash, I want you to start using checks and credit cards, so that you have records of your actual spending. Similarly, I want you to sock away some extra cash that you do not have to account for. Those are ways where you can camouflage some of the high spending.

If you are currently working, just hang tight with that job. Your income is already documented and you can't change that. If you are not working right now, then continue to NOT work, but do a few things to make it look like you are trying to find a job. A judge is likely to find more favor in your case, if you can produce a current copy of your resume and some date-stamped print outs of online job submissions. Even go on a few interviews and make note of that in your date book. However, do NOT go out and get a fancy, high-paying job. No, no, no. We do not need anyone to know what your earning potential is right now. We don't even want them to know which professional field you may be considering. Pick up a few odd jobs here and there, but refrain from claiming a steady, decent income. You may not want to – or have to – go back to work. You may want to go back to school. You may be better served staying home with the children. Start thinking about what you might want to do in the future, but refrain from making any changes to your income. And – keep this in mind – spousal support may be modified in the future. Your spouse can take you back to court and prove that you no longer need his support, if he discovers that you can support yourself!

Thus, "The Game"; contradictions in everyday behavior. You want to be independent, yet you must appear dependent. You want to cut back on your lifestyle, yet you must continue to look like you require the manner in which you were previously living. You pride yourself on truthful, ethical methods, yet you must be crafty and deceitful. You must embellish the simple. You must withhold the evidence. You must be covert and secretive. You must dart and dodge, bite your tongue, and plan a careful course over time.

Poker players who win have a good game face. If you cannot play poker, then stay silent and have your lawyer play the game for you. Remain silent. If your spouse wants to engage you in a discussion when you drop off Johnny, just say "We'll have to talk about this later." Or "You'll have to talk to my lawyer." Do not freely give away the intricacies of your case. You must keep your trump cards to yourself. You cannot get emotional and make demands of your ex-spouse because then he will know what is important to you. You may or may not have legal rights to make those claims, or your claims might just not be important to the other side and you have announced that they are!!! Again, it's a "game". You have a better chance at winning the game, if you keep your mouth shut about your desired outcome until the end of the process.

Sleuthing is a must. Uncover, carefully store, and do not divulge your knowledge of your ex's secrets. Keep track of things that your friends and children say about your spouse's whereabouts and conversations. You never know when this information might be useful. You must carefully look through and keep track of any inconsistencies that you might find in the set of documents that your ex delivers in his Discovery.

Investigating and uncovering the true facts about the marital finances are a necessity. But keep to yourself about whatever you might find!! Like I said in the previous chapters, you will need to first <u>gain access</u> to whatever financial statements that you can, and then <u>carefully review</u> the information (and start by looking at your taxes!), and then <u>make notes</u> about whatever details that seem significant to you. Whatever information you could not find out on your own will likely show up when your ex delivers his Discovery. And your lawyer has ways to check for other items that he does not disclose, so don't worry. When my ex produced his Discovery at my lawyer's office, I was shocked. There were accounts and business ventures that I had never heard of. He had started to have financial statements delivered to his office so I wouldn't see them. Instead of bringing home his paycheck, he'd stop at the bank and take out cash so I wouldn't know what the complete deposit was to be. He invested his commission check in risky business ventures, something I knew nothing about. And he altered the transactions in the QuickBooks account at his office. My lawyer was able to trace the transactions through the electronic log that is kept by the software. A trump card, indeed!

Instead of **reacting**, I held my emotions and actions close to my chest. I could have blown up at him and sent him a nasty e-mail or phone call explaining what I really thought of him. I was stunned. I was hurt and angry. But my legal team now had a game piece to use in the negotiations. We could not reveal that we had uncovered some of his secrets. Instead, my lawyer just slid a piece of paper across the table that highlighted the QuickBooks transactions. We held clear proof that he had misrepresented some financial information. The element of surprise was now ours and he could no longer stand firm in his negotiations. It took resolve and patience on my part, but it was part of the game.

Another aspect of the game of winning is to keep your long-term plans and goals a secret. You may not know what or where you will be in 10 or 20 years. You might want to spend some time thinking about it. Create a spreadsheet in Excel and make rows of categories against columns of time periods. Some helpful milestones might be one year, five years, ten years, and twenty-five years. Or use milestone ages for yourself, but be sure to include "retirement" as one of your milestones. Some categories of rows to think about: your home and location; your kids; employment; travel and entertainment; the balance in your retirement account; and whether you might remarry.

Massage these ideas over time, but do not let anyone know the emphasis on your life's priorities. In my case, I did not want my spouse to know that I planned to move to another state with a much lower cost of living. I needed the calculations for my spousal support to be based on the big city expenses of my current location. I purposely did not move until my divorce had settled for this reason. And, had I been asked about my plans, I would have lied. I certainly did not need for any conditions to be placed on my alimony, so I kept that information to myself. You might need to keep a potential inheritance or job to yourself. You might really want to remarry sooner, rather than later (or never). No matter what your goal for post-divorce life is, the fewer people you tell, the better. You will know in your heart the best way to achieve those goals. You do not want anyone to prevent you from following your heart.

Real-time access to joint assets is another part of the game and it can be frustrating for the non-working spouse. The wage-earning spouse can prevent you from access to the cash you need to pay your lawyer in the hopes that you may consider spending less on good counsel and thus, settle for less. In my case, I needed my lawyer to send out subpoenas and hire a forensic accountant in order to uncover the secret assets that were to be half mine. This required a great deal of money up front because I had to pay for services rendered each month. My lawyer was able to file a motion that released some joint money equally to both of us for legal expenses, but it did not even begin to cover the work I needed done. My husband was working and was able to pay his lawyer from his earnings; I did not have a pool of earnings to work from and I had to borrow money from my father. Without the loan from my father, I would have had no other choice but to resign myself to a lesser settlement.

I wish that I had been wiser during the separation because my ex played one aspect of the game that I didn't know about. Once we were legally separated, I should have filed for Separate Maintenance right away. It was an "amicable" separation and we both kept using the joint checking account the way we always had. It was a few months before I realized that he had stopped depositing his paycheck into our joint bank account. He wasn't required to legally, and he also did not have to tell me when he was no longer doing so. I thought commissions were slow, and I (as well as he) began to draw off of the home equity line of credit to pay living expenses. I was now living off of joint debt, debt that would now come off of my bottom line, instead of filing a petition for him to pay me temporary spousal support, money that would have been mine, and mine alone. Whichever side of the coin you are on regarding spousal support, make sure you understand how Pendente Lite works for providing temporary support (alimony) until your divorce is finalized. It could prove to be worth a great deal of money that will go unnoticed.

The negotiation of the division of assets is the final aspect of "the game", so make sure that your lawyer is a skilled negotiator. It can be an item-by-item "his" or "hers" kind of thing, or it can be a carefully crafted proposal. Be sure to create a spreadsheet of line items that you want considered in the negotiations. Make a note of the item description and value, and highlight whether or not it is something that you want. You need to also make a note of whether you think your spouse will want something. Create a "scale" of importance of items valuable to you and valuable to your spouse. Items that carry a highly charged emotional attachment are especially important. Often, it is not actually the dollar amount associated with an item that proves its value, but the sentimental or emotional attachment.

In the end, it really does not matter who gets the dining room set (unless it was your grandmother's!). You can always buy another one that you might like even better. Often times, your previous furnishings do not fit in your new home, you find that the item brings back too many memories, or your new spouse doesn't like it. Trust me, your taste will change. And there are so many things in life that we can honestly live without.

The fair division of assets may be a total dollar amount allocation or a lot of compromises on this and that. Your settlement may involve "conditions", "permissions", and "durations". Watch these carefully because they may restrict your life goals, and they also have a dollar value. For example, if you give your ex the rights to use the vacation home for one week every year, even though you will actually own it, you have not only tied yourself to the hassle of dealing with your ex over the timing and using of it, you may have lost one week's rental income. If your spouse wants to live in the marital home until the kids graduate from high school, be sure to do the math calculations on the dollar cost to you. Factor in the mortgage payments and home maintenance, and be sure to consider the sales market risks. Place a dollar amount "condition", should your agreement not be met. I allowed my ex to live in the marital home as long as he sold or refinanced it by a certain date. I essentially settled my half of the value of the home at the time of the divorce. We decided on a price and I no longer had to worry about the mortgage, the maintenance, negotiating with a realtor and the sales price, or showing it to potential buyers. If he did not meet the deadline to sell it or refinance it, he had to pay me $1500 each month until he did so. He was emotionally attached to the house and I was glad to be rid of it.

You can lump things together to help camouflage the emotional or valuable items. I thought that we were going to spend a lot of time and effort during my mediation going line by line on certain tangible items. I thought we were going to tick off "He gets the piano", "She gets the antique rocker". I was surprised to find that (since I had marked little interest on my spreadsheet) my lawyer went straight to negotiating a lump sum for the total of items and we just massaged a total dollar figure vs. ownership of things. At first I was a bit baffled since there seemed to be so many things left to haggle over. But I was pleasantly surprised that I essentially got a dollar amount for things I didn't want to own and didn't have to figure out how to move or sell! Again, the dollar value, but also the emotional/mental value was factored in. I had to trust my lawyer's negotiation skills.

I gave up on being short-sided and emotional. I had to let go and trust my gut.

There are a whole variety of ways to get creative with the final settlement. My spouse didn't need any more itemized deductions on his taxes, so we negotiated tax-free alimony for me. As the overall dollar figure settlement was being massaged, we craftily added another year of spousal support to my agreement. My ex was so busy watching the large dollar figures, he didn't really pay attention that **1 year** was really **12 times** a monthly dollar amount. And he agreed to "non-modifiable" spousal support. That meant that he could not take me back to court to reduce the spousal support amount if I decided to get a job. I've mentioned this before. Be sure to fully research and understand the conditions surrounding spousal support payments.

Health care and tax obligations also carry dollar and emotional value. Health insurance coverage and premiums may be more robust for or more essential for one spouse or the other. Make sure that you can validate medical coverage and the cost of that coverage once you are no longer covered by a family plan. IRS refunds, carry-overs, and capital gains are all dollar amounts that affect married couples. Be sure that you understand what these mean and how they affect you. You may agree to file joint taxes for another calendar year to save money, as well.

The bottom line is that you must be very knowledgeable and then quick on your feet during the negotiations. Remove as many of your emotional barriers as you can. Keep your long-range plan fresh in your mind. Be frugal and practical about your financial goals. Do not hang onto meaningless things just because of anger or resentment. If you have adequately prepared your lawyer, you can let him or her speak and negotiate on your behalf. Learn to play the game with a calm confidence and you will emerge victorious.

Notes

Notes

_____

_____

_____

_____

_____

_____

_____

_____

_____

_____

_____

_____

_____

CHAPTER ELEVEN:
THE LEGAL PROCESS –
What it might look like

Each state has different laws governing separation and divorce. And every divorce has its own particular aspects. And if children are involved, the laws will be very clear regarding their protection.

I want to give you a general idea of what your divorce process might look like in the hopes of enhancing your preparation and reducing your anxiety. My lawyer was not good at holding my hand and walking me through the milestones. She makes a living of settling divorces and does it all the time. It was a routine set of court filings and motions for her. She did not need to prepare herself emotionally, like I did. I knew that I had to trust my lawyer and the process, but I could have managed my stress and anxiety better, had I known what the full course of steps to a settlement were.

Some important aspects of your divorce can be settled prior to the final settlement. For example, you and your spouse can agree to a custody arrangement. You can agree to any number of things that you need to resolve, if both parties are in agreement.

Legal separation.
My ex and I began our journey with a legal separation. You do not have to move out of the house in order to file for a separation. I moved to sleeping in a separate bedroom and I found an attorney who could draw up a simple separation document. Even though we were interacting very little as a married couple, I needed to establish a DATE for which we could claim we were physically separated. Some states

93

require six months, others a year, of official separation before they will grant a divorce. In case my divorce would be settled quickly (it wasn't), I wanted to set a time-date stamp as timely as I could. Basically, a separation involves formally setting up new parameters on your relationship with your spouse to:

A.   Occupy separate bedrooms;
B.   Not share any romantic or sexual intimacy;
C.   Stop wearing wedding rings;
D.   Cease socializing together (e.g. will not attend parties, movies, theater, etc. together);
E.   With respect to the children, interact as parents only where strictly necessary from the children's perspective and their well being; e.g. it would be acceptable to go together to a meeting with a school official relative to problems confronting one of the children, but less appropriate to ride together and sit together at a school play or sporting event;
F.   Cease giving gifts to each other for birthdays, Christmas, anniversary, Valentines Day, etc.; and
G.   Make it known to close associates, relatives, etc. that we are martially separated within the residence, though continuing to reside under the same roof.

It is important to note that in Paragraph G, someone other than you or your spouse will eventually be required to sign an affidavit attesting to the validity of your separation.

Note: Once the Separation Date is determined and documented, any income and debts accumulated after that date belong to the individual, not the couple.

Filing legal documents with the court.
Over the course of your separation and divorce, both legal teams will file a variety of official documents with the court.

Both you and your spouse, as well as both lawyers, will always receive a copy of these documents.

If you are the first to file legal documents and start the divorce process, then you will be labeled the Plaintiff. The plaintiff is simply the person who makes the decision to bring a situation before a court of law. The other person in the divorce is called the Defendant. The defendant is required by law to *respond* to the plaintiff's *complaint* (see definitions below).

"Motions" are exactly that. They are court documents that set an idea or procedure in motion. They technically "ask for help". You will file a formal Motion for Divorce. You might file a motion for exclusive use of the marital home or the family car. You might file a motion for separate maintenance (temporary spousal support). You may likely file a motion for advancement of legal fees. I had to file a "Motion to Compel" several times to get my spouse to actually provide what was requested in a prior motion. We filed a motion to agree on which realtor to use and what asking price when we needed to put the marital home on the market. Your lawyer will determine and file whatever motions he or she deems necessary.

Note: Motions almost always ask for the legal fees spent to generate the Motion be paid by the other party. This seems to be a standard cover-your-ass, scare tactic. In my divorce, it seemed like I was always being asked to pay for my ex's Motions. The request for fees is usually the last paragraph of a legal document and it sounds as though your ex is saying this: "I can't believe that I have to spend money to fight you on this. I'm going to win this argument and you are going to have to pay for it after I win!" Not to worry. Your legal documents will say the same thing to your ex as you file them. I am not sure how often these threats are followed through on, but it seems to be standard practice. I never had to pay my ex for any of the motions he filed against me!

Here is a general idea of what some of the legal documents mean:

- Affidavit – sworn statement
- Answer – different from a Response, this is the first document filed by the defendant to a Complaint. If the defendant's lawyer does not file an Answer, the court might enter judgment against the defendant.
- Complaint – initiates action by outlining the facts and causes of the issue and then suggests resolution to those issues
- Motion – ask for help
- Objection – opposing something
- Petition – states certain facts of the case
- Request – a direction or command served upon the other party
- Response – part of the fact-finding process during Discovery, a Response to a Request must be produced by the other party within a certain time limit
- Suit – an action brought before a court of law by one party against another
- Summons – commands a spouse to do certain things

Pendente Lite.

During the separation period, you will file a Motion for Pendente Lite Relief that will establish your finances for the interim period. The Complaint for Separate Maintenance will ensure that you are financially supported with temporary child support and/or alimony until the divorce is finalized. Both your lawyer and your spouse's lawyer will send out a document that requests some detailed information about your current income and expenses. You will also go over your children's interim needs, especially if there are some unusual expenses involved with their health or activities. The documents that you will be required to provide will be related to your current everyday expenses.

You will need to create an accurate income and expense (I/E) sheet (see **Figure 1**). Your lawyer should walk you through what each of the line items mean and how to calculate or estimate an accurate figure. Pay attention to how the calculations are determined since you will be required to update the I/E report again, closer to the divorce settlement.

Monthly Income and Expenses of _____ Date: _____

Complaint #. _____

Employed By	
City & State	
Occupation	
Pay Period	
Next Payday	
Salary/Wage	
# Exemptions	

Children in Household

Name	Age

Average Gross Pay per Month	
LESS: Federal Taxes	
State Taxes	
FICA	
Health Insurance	
Life Insurance	
Required Retirement	
Average Monthly Net Pay	
Other Income	
MONTHLY NET INCOME	

Household
- Mortgage (PITI) or Rent
- Real Estate Property Taxes
- Homeowner's Insurance
- Repairs/Maintenance
- Furniture/Furnishings

Utilities
- Electricity
- Gas/Heating Oil
- Water/Sewer
- Telephone
- Trash
- Cable TV

Food
- Groceries
- Lunches

Automobile
- Payment/Depreciation
- Gasoline
- Repair/Tags/Inspection, etc.
- Auto Insurance
- Parking/Other Transportation
- Personal Property Tax

Childcare Expenses
- Child Care
- School Tuition
- Lunch Money
- School Supplies
- Lessons/Sports
- New Clothing

Clothing
- New (Excluding Children)
- Cleaning/Laundry
- Uniforms

Health Expenses
- Doctor
- Dentist
- Therapist
- Eyeglasses
- Hospital
- Medicines
- Other

Dues
- Professional Associations
- Social Associations
- Homeowner's Association

Miscellaneous
- Gifts (Xmas,Birthday)
- Church/Charity
- Entertainment
- Vacations
- Hobbies
- Personal Grooming
- Newspaper/Magazines
- Disability Insurance
- Life Insurance
- Legal Expenses

Totals Per Month
- Subtotal Expenses
- Subtotal Debt Payments
- TOTAL EXPENSES
- TOTAL NET INCOME
- BALANCE (+)
- BALANCE (-)

Fixed Debts with Payments	Balance	Mo. Pmt.

Charge Account Debt		

Liquid Assets on Hand
- Cash/Checking/Savings
- Other Liquid Assets
- TOTAL LIQUID ASSETS

Submitted By: _____

Figure 1 Income and Expense Sheet

The finances that are set up during Pendente Lite are usually based on percentage guidelines. Different states have different guidelines and temporary support is based on the amount of income involved. Temporary child support is also determined based on a guideline. Your lawyers should be able to resolve this issue quickly and without lengthy discussion because the amounts that are to be appropriated are generally determined according to state guidelines and are only temporary.

The Discovery Process - Interrogatories and Requests for Documentation.

After the interim finances are sorted out, then you will begin the process of sorting through all of the long-term, detailed information for your divorce settlement. Your lawyer will file a document to change your Complaint for Separate Maintenance to a Divorce Suit and you and your ex will likely be mandated to attend a divorce education class.

Both lawyers will send out a detailed set of Interrogatories and Request for Documentation to the other person. Each of you will get your own set of these legal documents. Interrogatories are a huge set of questions for you and your spouse to answer. Essentially, your ex is interrogating you for the record. And you are doing the same!

For the set of Interrogatories and Request for Documentation that you send to your ex, make sure that your lawyer's request covers *all* areas of assets that you want full disclosure on. The questions and requests ask for basic information about current accounts and balances, joint assets, etc., as well as a statement of why you feel the marriage has failed. Make sure that your lawyer covers other general categories (i.e., business ventures, trusts, inheritances, promissory notes), in case there is something out there that you are not aware of. Do not just ask for the stuff that you already know about! Your lawyer is limited in the number of items that he/she can ask for. Be sure to review the Interrogatories and Request for Documentation before your lawyer sends them to your ex.

The Request for Documentation will be just that. You must provide (usually for the past five years) documents that support all of your answers to the Interrogatories. Similar to what I mentioned earlier about asking the questions, be sure to ask for any and all documents that you might need to have.

Collecting all of your documents and formulating all of your answers is exhausting. It's time-consuming and mentally draining. Some of the questions that you might have to answer are insulting or embarrassing. Try not to take it personally. Remember it's a process. It's a game, a challenge. Hopefully, your ex is finding the process equally as challenging. Chances are, one of the lawyers drafted the first set of Interrogatories and the opposing lawyer used the same set of questions with little differentiation. You are generally both answering the same type of questions.

Your lawyer should be able to provide you with an electronic version of the Interrogatories document to type your answers into. If he or she does not offer the electronic copy, be sure to ask for it. It will save you a lot of money, if you can do the typing yourself. Take your time and save often. If you don't know the answer, make some notes and come back to that question later. Since you will have to provide supporting documentation for all of your answers, begin to organize and collate the documents as you refer to them. You will have to look up and provide all financial account numbers. It is important that your lawyer review all of your answers and documents prior to submission.

Subpoenas.

Your divorce may require that you send out some subpoenas duces tecum (SDTs) to gather information from the actual source. SDTs are fact-finding treasure hunts. They can be expensive, if the person you are requesting the information from charges for their time or copying costs. The person being served finds them a complete nuisance. Subpoenas are also intrusive and embarrassing. They give the impression of distrust or foul play. They send a message to the opposing side that you do not trust the complete or accurate disclosure of their Discovery. While the primary purpose of SDTs is to uncover factual information, SDTs also emotionally manipulate and unnerve the opposing side by playing into potential shame or guilt. And they are definitely embarrassing to your ex because someone that they do business with is being put out some time and energy on their behalf just because of a divorce.

Depositions.

Your divorce may also involve something called a deposition. Depositions can be costly, but they can also give your case justification and proof for any suspected wrongdoing or motive. The deposition of a person is taken with both lawyers present and a court reporter that provides a written transcript. In my divorce, my lawyer conducted a deposition of my husband's business partner who admitted under oath that he had been hiding money for my ex. Imagine how victorious it felt to have that knowledge about the opposition!

Again, be kind to yourself. The Discovery process takes weeks. Take breaks. Don't beat yourself up if you cannot locate some of the records. Ask a friend to help with copying, organizing, and labeling things. You may have to spend some time redacting the account numbers (crossing through all but the last four numbers in an account identifier). You will need to make at least one copy of the documents, but most likely two or three. When you make the copies, make *single-sided* copies of everything and do not use staples. You may want to purchase an inexpensive scanner and create electronic files of everything.

As I mentioned before about handling all of the documents, be discreet. You do not want your children to see any of the documents, nor be a party to how much effort you are exerting. They do not need the added stress. Stay organized. Glance at the documents as they go through the copy machine feeder. Marry up important dates and facts. Some documents may look different from what you remembered. Some documents may look completely foreign! Familiarize yourself with them. Be prepared to locate something quickly.

Preparing for your settlement negotiations.

Once you receive your spouse's Discovery documents, you will need to make a copy for yourself. Inventory and organize them and familiarize yourself with them. Create a spreadsheet with the Interrogatory question, his answer, and the documents that were provided. Do they adequately answer all of the questions? Are there any surprises? Check important dates, withdrawals, and deposits. Review his credit card statements carefully because they tell a history of whereabouts and activity. Be sure to inform your lawyer of any concerns you may have.

If you haven't already done so, you really need to familiarize yourself with your tax returns. If you have to go back farther than five years, then do so. You will need to compare the adjusted gross income of the years. Look at capital gains, deductions, and interest. Make notes of home purchases and sales. You will end up haggling about who owned which assets prior to when you got married.

Mediation.

There are lots of different ways to come to the results of a divorce settlement now. The primary method that proves results is through Mediation. You may start the process with one lawyer sending a low-ball settlement offer over to the other lawyer. The initial offer is always insulting. Do not take it personally. It's a game. It's a business deal. Everyone wants to save money (retain money) any way that they can! You may set up informal meetings to try to resolve some sticky issues.

Formal mediation is set up between your lawyers. They set up parameters ahead of time so that you can meet the goals of time and effort. In my divorce, we set up a Mediation session with a retired judge. We paid the retired judge to help us settle our case. We both agreed that the judge was impartial and that we would accept his judgment, based on his prior experience settling divorce cases. On the day that we met for mediation, we met with and signed a contract with the judge attesting to this. My lawyer ensured that my ex and I had separate rooms to process the offer of settlement that went back and forth between us. We brought all of our paperwork, a laptop, and snacks. My lawyer maintained an electronic copy of the actual settlement and made updates to the document as things were settled and agreed to. We signed the agreed upon document before we left the office.

Mediation is nerve-wracking. Your future is being settled. It requires patience and self-care. If you need breaks to collect your thoughts, be sure to take them. Call a friend. Ignore the insulting offers. Don't take anything personally. Trust your lawyer and her negotiating skills. My lawyer had a few trump cards up her sleeve and she used them when it was necessary. I had prepared her very carefully and she knew what he would likely ask for, so she was prepared to refute his claims and counter his offers. Now is not the time to be nice – or generous.

Trial.

If you have to take your case to court to settle the differences between you and your spouse, then expect it to be expensive. There are court fees and filing fees, as well as your lawyer's bill. You risk the luck of the draw with which judge is appointed to hear your case. The judge's personality and your lawyer's rapport with that judge are definitely factors. If you must settle in court, make sure that you sit in on a few unrelated court proceedings at the courthouse to learn more about the environment you will be placed in. Your lawyer should walk you through the process and educate you on the possible outcome.

Notes

_____

_____

_____

_____

_____

_____

_____

_____

_____

_____

_____

_____

_____

_____

Notes

_____

_____

_____

_____

_____

_____

_____

_____

_____

_____

_____

_____

_____

_____

CHAPTER TWELVE:
THE NEGOTIATION

The results of your final settlement are ultimately your responsibility. Your lawyer only has so many skills and so much knowledge about your case. That is why it is imperative that you educate your lawyer with the history of your case, the present state of your assets, and your wants and desires for the future. No detail is insignificant. Even if your desired outcome seems unreachable, your lawyer must know what you are ultimately seeking.

You need to do the prep work. It's exhausting. It's worth it. Your future depends on it. You, yourself, need to research and educate yourself about the financial patterns of your previous married life. You need to read and understand your taxes. And you need to do some soul-searching about what you want in the future. Do you want to have all of your money up front? Do you want your financial settlement spread out over several years? Do you want to remarry? Do you want to work or go back to school?

Establish your goals.

Create a spreadsheet for your goals. Make columns for one year from now, five years from now, twenty years from now, and retirement. Make applicable rows of goals for yourself. Be sure to include a row for: housing; retirement savings; employment; concerns for each of your children; a romantic relationship; etc. Massage and update the spreadsheet over several months. You will be surprised at how your values and goals will change over time, especially as your shock and anger (hopefully) dissipates. Be sure to check your motives for your goals. Is it something you really want to pursue in life, or have you marked it down just to spite your ex? Is it something you *want* to do in life, or something you feel like you *should* do because of someone else's expectations?

Review the risks of the goals on your spreadsheet, as well. Are you fighting to claim an asset (such as the vacation house) that might be difficult to maintain or sell in the future, if you change your mind? Are your goals clouded by sentiment, trauma, or others' opinions? Are you sure that your children *really* **want** that for you? Your lawyer is likely not to question your emotions regarding the settlement. That is why it is important to review your desired settlement outcome with a trusted friend or family member prior to beginning the negotiations. A disinterested third-party will be able to point out the flaws in your thought-process. They can point out the ramifications associated with a line item, or the long-term benefit or risk associated with a line item. A second opinion is especially helpful if you are experiencing any shame or remorse for behavior leading up to the failed marriage. Even the person "at fault", so to speak, deserves a fair settlement.

Clearly identify the assets and obligations.
As you near the final settlement meeting, you will need to create a spreadsheet of assets to be distributed between the two of you. For each line item, create a column of its emotional or dollar value; supporting history or evidence (or where to locate the information); and your thoughts on how it should be divided. You can manipulate the spreadsheet into dollar amount summaries and "his" and "hers", so that you can look at the entire estate from all angles. Share this information with your legal team and strategize a plan to resolve all issues. What do you anticipate to be the difficult issues? What are the non-issues? What are your "must haves"? What are your trump cards?

With your goals for the details of the final settlement in hand and your long-range plans for your future clear in your head, you will be well-prepared to confidently embark on the negotiations. If you are well prepared, you will also have time to manage your stress and emotions. Be sure to get a good night's sleep and good nutrition. Take breaks.

Never try to handle the negotiations on your own. Never make verbal or written offers or conditions to your spouse directly. You might be making false claims, emotional decisions, or giving away your trump cards! Your lawyer will handle the process itself. He or she is skilled in the timing of negotiation techniques – when to play fair, when to withhold, when to stand firm, when to call the bluff.

Most likely, you will settle on the easy things first. Hopefully, you have previously already settled on child custody issues. Your lawyer will develop a sales and marketing strategy for the remainder. My lawyer completely ignored the "line items" I gave her (since there were so many line items that I really didn't care about) and went straight to an offer that involved an overall dollar settlement, resolution on the marital home, and her idea of years of spousal support. I was stunned, since I thought we were going to decide on the grand piano and oriental rugs! Instead of going through each nickel and dime, she knew that my ex would negotiate better at a high level. I had prepared her well. I had accurately described my spouse's mannerisms and personality. And I had limited my emotions, my "must haves", to very few tangible assets. At that point, it was just about money and my future goals.

We brought all of our supporting documentation, a laptop, drinks and snacks to the mediation location. My lawyer's assistant kept an evolving draft of the settlement on a word processor and made changes and final edits to the document real-time. Between the three of us, we were able to verify the accuracy of the language as it was settled upon, and the final draft was ready to print and sign before anyone had a chance to change their mind on the conditions.

You need to read every word of the divorce settlement before you sign it. Each "or", "and", and "however" means something. Do the math. Small dollar figures could add up to a great deal of cash when then multiplied by twelve months or five years. Verify dates and check them against your master personal plan. Payments may be set up for any date that works for you or your ex, not necessarily January 1st.

Make sure that you have someone advise you on the tax ramifications of your divorce. You may save money by filing jointly again this final year. You may use your *willingness* to file jointly as a means for negotiation. You may use prior tax carryovers, deductions, or capital gains as a means for negotiation.

My ex-husband was in business for himself and our taxes were very complex. As it turned out, he really didn't need any more itemizations for tax deductions, so my lawyer set up my alimony to be tax-free. She placed a provision in the settlement that, should he change his mind on wanting to use the tax deduction for spousal support, he would then have to increase my monthly amount. I had no idea that you could set up such a strategy. This was something that made sense for both of us. Make sure that you are always watching for solutions and compromises that are win-win.

Try to plan for every scenario, especially in the case of minor children. Medical expenses for any family member are always an unknown risk and an unforeseen condition or accident could end up being very costly. Make sure that you try to plan for any of your children's special needs, such as specialized training or instruction, private school, or summer plans. Even summer camp, or extended time at home during off-school periods can be expensive. You are not required to negotiate and settle on issues for adult children who are legally emancipated at age 18. Only discuss issues concerning adult children, if there are extenuating circumstances or savings/trust money allocated in their name.

The back and forth negotiations may last hours, or days. Be patient. Don't take it personally. The first set of offers will be insulting. Insulting to your time invested in the marital relationship, and insulting to your intelligence. Wait it out. Trust your lawyer. Trust your gut. Trust your long-range plan. Don't settle because you are emotionally or physically worn down. Stay focused and pay attention to every detail. Try to focus on the end result.

Remember: "This, too, shall pass." Everything always does.

Notes

_____

_____

_____

_____

_____

_____

_____

_____

_____

_____

_____

_____

_____

_____

_____

CHAPTER THIRTEEN:
POST-DIVORCE –
GOING BACK TO COURT

We are now in the age where legal litigation is commonplace. People sue people all the time. I want you to be aware that you or your ex-spouse can file a motion against one another at any time, even though your divorce is settled and finalized. Either you or your ex can claim a **Change in Circumstance**, if your lawyer feels it is warranted.

Your divorce settlement is reached and finalized based on the current and accurate state of affairs at that time. In the months and years following your settlement, things can change. You could find that you are having difficulties with your child(ren) in academics, substance abuse, mental illness, physical illness or accident, or custodial issues. You may have trouble maintaining or selling the marital home. You or your ex may have a dramatic change in employment; both the loss of a job, or securing a new high-paying job creates changes in the previously settled divorce finances. These are all unforeseen events that could not be planned for at the time of your divorce settlement.

Any and all modifications to child support must be done through the court system. Neither you, nor your ex, can modify the monthly dollar amount of child support that was previously determined in your divorce process without going through the legal system.

If you have a good lawyer and you believe that you anticipate an issue of some sort in the future, you may be able to thwart a potential law suit by carefully drafting language with "or" or "however" clauses. One of my children was in counseling at the time of my divorce and my lawyer drafted a lengthy paragraph that stated my ex was to be responsible for all of my child's medical expenses ("including psychiatrists, psychologists, prescriptions, hospitals, etc."). It turned out that, after the divorce was settled, my child required a great deal of help from mental health professionals and I was glad that we could hold my ex to such robust terms. We also placed conditions on the marital home. If it did not sell by a certain date, my ex was required to pay me an extra dollar amount each month until it sold. Without this clause, my ex really had no clear motivation to sell the house and he could have stalled or played games with me regarding this issue. Try to anticipate as many "if ...thens..." as you can!

As I've mentioned before, seek professional advice prior to securing a good job in the workplace. If you have agreed in your settlement to *conditional* alimony, your ex has every right to take you back to court to stop paying you once it is determined that you can adequately support yourself. One of my friends was a stay-at-home mother and decided to go back to work, even though her children were still in elementary school. She needed the extra money. She felt that she could manage the work schedule and still care for her children. However, that goal of having extra money quickly evaporated. Her ex sued her based on this Change in Circumstance and she lost her alimony. She could have stayed home and spent time with her children for the same amount of money as that new high-powered job. A part-time job for some extra spending money might not have indicated to the other side that she could adequately support herself. It's a personal decision, obviously. I just want you to be aware of the risks associated with your earning potential.

It really sucks, if he is the one suing you, so be sure to remember how to play the game. It plays out just like a mini-divorce, with motions, Discovery and Interrogatories, SDTs, release of all financial information, and more legal bills. You will have to act as though you do not have a lot of money again. You will have to monitor your words and actions and keep your side of the street clean. Make sure that you keep an emergency fund of money for just this type of unforeseen "event".

Notes

_____

_____

_____

_____

_____

_____

_____

_____

_____

_____

_____

_____

_____

CHAPTER FOURTEEN:
STAY EMPOWERED

This book is intended to empower you to successfully navigate a divorce. Hopefully, the motivation to become empowered will help you to become your best self yet! It's like the stewardess on an airline that states at the beginning of every flight: "Be sure to put on your own oxygen mask first before helping others." Don't be lazy about your own self-care. Get empowered – and stay empowered!

You have access to all kinds of free and inexpensive help, you just need to know where to look for it. Your county government division of social services is a good place to start. The government provides shelters and services for all kinds of people and these places often provide free workshops and pro bono (free) advice. Use the Internet to search your county government website.

You can basically type any kind of search into your browser and find unlimited resources. Type buzzwords or questions into the browser and see what comes up!

I am a HUGE fan of Suzy Orman when it comes to learning how to manage your personal finances. In my opinion, she is the financial empowering "guru". She has written countless books, and she has a television show and a very robust, empowering website. You can find her books at any bookstore. Specifically, <u>Women and Money</u>, <u>Suzie Orman's Action Plan</u>, and <u>The 9 Steps to Financial Freedom</u> are especially good at outlining good solid financial advice. Suzie Orman does not skimp when it comes to overcoming shame and guilt about managing your money. She is especially skilled at helping you to overcome your financial fears. Check out her website at <u>www.suzieorman.com</u>. The website has free articles and blogs, and hyperlinks you to any number of other financial resources, depending on your interest. It's all there – anything you want to know about money!

I wish you the best of luck with your journey to uncover your best self. My own journey to happiness was lengthy and exhausting, but I made it safely to the other side. I want you to know that **you can, too!**

Notes

You Can, Too by Rosie Woods

You Can, Too by Rosie Woods

_____

_____

_____

_____

_____

_____

_____

_____

_____

_____

_____

_____

_____

_____

_____

_____

_____

_____

_____

_____

_____

_____

_____

_____

_____

_____

_____

_____

Index

www.ingramcontent.com/pod-product-compliance
Lightning Source LLC
LaVergne TN
LVHW021348080426
835508LV00020B/2160